Using Discussion to Promote Reading Comprehension

Donna E. Alvermann
University of Georgia

Deborah R. Dillon
David G. O'Brien
Purdue University

Published by the
International Reading Association
Newark, Delaware 19714

INTERNATIONAL READING ASSOCIATION

OFFICERS
1987-1988

President   Phylliss J. Adams, University of Denver, Denver, Colorado

Vice President   Patricia S. Koppman, PSK Associates, San Diego, California

Vice President Elect   Dale D. Johnson, Instructional Research and Development Institute, Boston, Massachusetts

Executive Director   Ronald W. Mitchell, International Reading Association, Newark, Delaware

DIRECTORS

Term Expiring Spring 1988
   Margaret Pope Hartley, The Psychological Corporation, North Little Rock, Arkansas
   P. David Pearson, University of Illinois, Champaign, Illinois
   Carol M. Santa, School District #5, Kalispell, Montana

Term Expiring Spring 1989
   Marie C. DiBiasio, Bristol Public Schools, Bristol, Rhode Island
   Hans U. Grundin, The Open University, Milton Keynes, England
   Nancy E. Seminoff, Winona State University, Winona, Minnesota

Term Expiring Spring 1990
   Jerome C. Harste, Indiana University, Bloomington, Indiana
   Jane M. Hornburger, Brooklyn College, CUNY, Brooklyn, New York
   Merrillyn Brooks Kloefkorn, Jefferson County Public Schools, Golden, Colorado

Copyright 1987 by the
International Reading Association, Inc.

Library of Congress Cataloging-in-Publication Data

Alvermann, Donna E.
   Using discussion to promote reading comprehension.
   Includes bibliographies.
   1. Content area reading—United States.   2. Discussion.
3. Reading comprehension. I. Dillon, Deborah R.   II.
O'Brien, David G.   III. Title.
LB1050.455.A48   1987   428.4'3   87-3107
ISBN 0-87207-787-X

Contents

Foreword   iv

Preface   vi

1   What Discussion Is and Is Not   1

2   The Role of Discussion in Promoting Reading
    Comprehension   9

3   The Influence of Context on Discussion Practices   14

4   Planning the Discussion   24

5   Discussion Strategies for Content Area Reading   34

6   Implementing the Discussion   43

7   Two Procedures for Evaluating Discussion   57

Carrie Rich Memorial Library
Campbell University
Buies Creek, N.C. 27506

190138

10-10-88 B4T $7.23 Ed-Under

iii

Foreword

Discussion can—and certainly should—be an important part of comprehension instruction. This publication, in clear and concise form, makes a strong case for using discussion as an important part of content area instruction. The monograph has a good balance between the *why* and the *how to* of classroom discussion in content area instruction.

Drawing from the writers' experiences in observing discussion in twenty-four different classrooms, Alvermann, Dillon, and O'Brien illustrate their major points with classroom transcripts of discussion in content area classes. Observations used come from a variety of areas, including social studies, science, and literature classes. It is refreshing to note in the transcripts of observations examples of the little glitches that keep much classroom instruction from being perfect. Critiques are offered to indicate how the teachers might have improved their performances to make their discussion sessions even more effective in helping students to comprehend and to be more effective discussants in content classes.

Among the unique features of the monograph (in addition to the actual classroom examples cited) are the clear distinction drawn between recitation and discussion, the attention given to the importance of physical arrangement of the classroom in discussion sessions, the importance of preplanning for effective instruction, and the emphasis on critical thinking as an important part of class discussion. Ample attention is given to each of these areas.

To encourage students to participate actively in meaningful discussion—and to have them feel comfortable in doing so—is a valuable avenue of instruction for content area teachers. However, such approaches are not necessarily easy for teachers to master. For the teacher who wants class activities to be teacher controlled and orchestrated, the kind of class discussion outlined can be downright uncomfortable. The writers, drawing from their own research and experiences in using discussion strategies, offer guides for teachers and teachers in preparation to help them gain expertise and security in the use of discussion in their content area classes. Further, teachers who now use classroom discussion as important parts of their instruction can gain additional ideas from the study of this monograph. Though the intended audiences for *Using Discussion to Promote Reading Comprehension* are middle school and secondary level content area teachers, many of the ideas apply equally well to lower grade levels and to developmental reading instruction.

Ira E. Aaron
Professor Emeritus
University of Georgia

Preface

*U*sing Discussion to Promote Reading Comprehension has a twofold purpose: to provide preservice and inservice teachers at the middle and high school levels with the motivation and knowledge necessary for using discussion to foster their students' comprehension of assigned textbook material and to share some research based reasons for incorporating the discussion method into an existing repertoire of teaching strategies. This monograph simultaneously addresses the *how to* and the *why* of using discussion to increase students' ability to comprehend what they read in content area texts.

We have used a number of sources to provide a context for what we have learned from observing teachers using discussion to promote reading comprehension in various subject areas. In Chapter 1, the distinctions between discussion and recitation are examined and major issues related to content area discussion are redefined in light of recent research and school reform reports.

Chapter 2 establishes a basis for the premise that discussion is important to the development of reading comprehension. Those skills that enrich or refine students' understanding of text are described and illustrated.

In Chapter 3, portions of transcripts from videotaped content area discussions are used to illustrate several factors of classroom context that influence discussion practices. Alternatives to teacher dominated discussions are described, and guidelines are provided for establishing the rights and responsibilities of critical readers.

Chapter 4 demonstrates how to plan for a classroom discussion of assigned content area materials. Five aspects of the planning process are described: specifying the objectives of a discussion, selecting content appropriate for a discussion, choosing discussion strategies that enrich or refine students' understanding of text, organizing the class for large or small group discussion, and evaluating the success of teaching with the discussion method.

Chapter 5 presents discussion strategies that help students master the content, examine more than one side of an issue, and evaluate alternative solutions to a text based problem. Each strategy is matched to an appropriate instructional purpose. The purpose, rationale, and steps in implementing each strategy are followed by examples of classroom use and limitations.

Chapter 6 analyzes one content area teacher's implementation of a pre-planned discussion. Commentaries follow each of several segments of a transcript taken from a videotaped classroom discussion. The commentaries include an analysis of what happened during the discussion, how and why the teacher/student interactions proceeded as they did, and suggestions for changes in those interactions.

Chapter 7 describes two procedures for informally evaluating class-room discussion used to promote reading comprehension. The first procedure, a bipolar evaluation of activities that change according to the instructional purpose for a discussion, can be used by teachers to develop profiles of their interaction patterns with students. The second procedure is useful for analyzing discussion activities that teachers use as followups to assigned content area reading.

DEA
DRD
DGO

IRA DIRECTOR OF PUBLICATIONS   Jennifer A. Stevenson

IRA PUBLICATIONS COMMITTEE 1987-1988   James E. Flood, San Diego State University, *Chair* • James F. Baumann, Purdue University • Janet R. Binkley, IRA • Phyllis E. Brazee, University of Maine • Susan W. Brennan, IRA • Kent L. Brown Jr., *Highlights for Children* • Marie DiBiasio, Bristol Public Schools, Bristol, Rhode Island • Dolores Durkin, University of Illinois • Philip Gough, University of Texas at Austin • Margaret K. Jensen, Madison Metropolitan School District, Madison, Wisconsin • John Micklos, Jr., IRA • Ronald W. Mitchell, IRA • Joy N. Monahan, Orange County Public Schools, Orlando, Florida • Allan R. Neilsen, Mount St. Vincent University • John J. Pikulski, University of Delaware • María Elena Rodríguez, IRA, Buenos Aires • Jennifer A. Stevenson, IRA • Anne C. Tarleton, Albuquerque Public Schools, Albuquerque, New Mexico

The International Reading Association attempts, through its publications, to provide a forum for a wide spectrum of opinions on reading. This policy permits divergent viewpoints without assuming the endorsement of the Association.

1

What discussion is and is not

T he purpose of this chapter is to define classroom discussion and to compare it with classroom recitation.

Discussion is important both as a communication skill and as a means for developing higher level reading skills. As a teaching method, discussion has been hailed as "the cornerstone of oral language work" during the middle school years (Corson, 1984, p. 30). For teachers and students at the high school level, discussion offers one of the few teaching and learning alternatives to the straight lecture method. Within the past decade a small body of research on discussion, which is separate from questioning research, has begun to surface. This research (see Dillon, 1984) is supplemented by more literature on discussion that includes opinions and recommended practices—the kind generally found in methods texts and practitioner journals.

The greatest source of information about classroom discussion is neither the research nor the applied literature but the discussion practices that skilled teachers use daily. This latter source of information forms the basis of the examples used in this book. The results of the eighteen months of observational study—involving twenty-four science, social studies, literature, health, and human development teachers in rural, suburban, and urban school districts—revealed a wide range of discussion practices (Alvermann et al., 1984). Most of the practices observed have been defined in the literature on teaching.

Multiple definitions of discussion

Some of the early pedagogical writers (Landon, 1899) equated discussion with the conversation method—an informal chat carried on in a free manner with no overt tones of formal instruction. Under this method, students were encouraged to converse freely, to say what they thought, and to question unfamiliar ideas. The teacher's role was one of directing and guiding students' thoughts by asking questions, often for the purpose of holding their attention.

A half century later, Bloom (1954, p. 38) described discussion as a "cooperative attack on a common set of problems, based on a common set of data, materials, and experiences, in which the problem is pursued to as complex and deep a level as possible." Although Stanford and Stanford (1969, p. 15) viewed discussion from a similar perspective, they added a dimension – "to gain feelings of acceptance and belonging."

In *Education, Democracy, and Discussion,* Bridges (1979, p. 16) posed what he termed necessary and sufficient conditions for specifying that individuals are engaged in a discussion. He stated that individuals "are putting forward more than one point of view upon a subject...[and] are at least disposed to examine and to be responsive to the different points of view put forward...with the intention of developing their knowledge, understanding, and/or judgment on the matter under discussion."

Recitation contrasted to discussion

According to Dillon (1984), recitation is a rubric covering activities that include reviewing, drilling, and quizzing. In the transcribed video dialogue below, students' answers reflect the health teacher's emphasis on recitation.

Setting *Students in an eighth grade health class read a portion of the chapter on poison control the day before the videotaping. In the beginning segment of the transcript, which was typical of the entire lesson, Ms. Sneed quizzed the class on their assigned reading.*

Sneed
All right, Vinny. Would you try to identify the poison for all victims or only the ones that are conscious?

Vinny
All victims.

Sneed
All victims. Good. Roger? Would you call the poison center for all victims or only the ones that are conscious?

Roger
All of them.

Sneed
All of them. Good. Lee? Would you treat for shock only those victims who are conscious or all victims?

Lee
All victims.

Sneed
All victims. Good. Would you watch to be sure that all victims keep breathing, Jeri, or only the conscious ones?

Jeri
All.

Dillon (1981) distinguished recitation from discussion by defining the criteria that characterize an interaction as a discussion. According to Dillon, if the teacher planned to have a discussion, if the students rated it as such, and if at least 40 percent of the total talk could be attributed to students, then the exchange was a discussion. This practical approach to judging whether a discussion has occurred makes sense. It also provides an easy index for teachers who wish to take a more careful look at their own classroom interaction patterns.

Based on the discussion observed, the discussion method is distinguishable from the recitation method on at least three different criteria: (1) the discussants must present multiple points of view and then be ready to change their minds after hearing convincing counterarguments; (2) the students must interact with one another as well as with the teacher; and (3) a majority of the verbal interactions, especially those resulting from questions that solicit student opinion, must be longer than the typical two or three word phrases found in recitations. In the transcribed video dialogue that follows, all three criteria are present.

Setting *Students in Mr. McKay's all male eighth grade human development class had been assigned to read a chapter on sexist beliefs and behaviors. As this segment of the dialogue opens, McKay is attempting to get Manny to elaborate on an earlier response and, in so doing, to change his opinion.*

McKay
All right, Manny, what form of prejudice do you have toward females? Give me an example. (long pause; Manny looks up at the ceiling) Do you think it's all right for a female to play on the football team?

Manny (hesitantly)
No, because they aren't as strong as...I mean they have a different body structure than men.

Sam
But suppose you have a female who is as strong as the strongest male player on the football team?

Manny
I think she'd do the same or maybe better. (pause) What's your opinion, Reginald?

Reginald
I think they can be equal in jobs and stuff, but I don't think they should play, you know. I can understand them playing baseball and soccer and maybe basketball. But I don't think they should play football. I wouldn't like it if they brought a woman into football.

McKay
A school in a neighboring county has a girl in football and she's strong.

Students (in unison)
In *football?*

McKay
Yes, she plays safety.

Instructional purposes of discussion

Discussion is a curricular task selected by content area teachers for a variety of reasons. Some teachers may perceive discussion as a forum in which important issues can be raised in relation to reading assignments; others may see discussion as an opportunity for identifying and clarifying students' misconceptions; still others may view discussion as a way of checking on who read the assigned material.

When teachers use the word *discuss* in a generic sense, as in "Read pages 29-36 and be ready to discuss the material tomorrow," students may be unclear about what is expected of them. A better approach is to alert students to the purpose or objective of the discussion.

Gall and Gall (1976) have classified discussions according to specific instructional objectives. For example, if *subject mastery* is the desired objective, teachers might alert students to be prepared to define terms and identify important concepts in the assigned material, to apply what they learn in their reading to other bodies of knowledge, or to evaluate the author's arguments.

A second instructional objective used by Gall and Gall is the intent to bring about a change in attitude, as in *issue oriented discussions*. Teachers who make content area reading assignments in anticipation of issue oriented discussions need to inform students to read to increase their awareness and understanding of others' beliefs and feelings about a particular topic. Issue oriented discussions also might be used to help students analyze or evaluate and, perhaps, modify their attitudes to be consistent with the results of their analyses and evaluations.

A third instructional purpose for a discussion, according to Gall and Gall, is to provide a public forum for *problem solving*. To use problem solving effectively within a textbook related discussion, students must read in depth about a topic or concept. If students lack the necessary background knowledge, a film, filmstrip, or videocassette describing others' solutions to a similar problem may serve as a stimulant to their own thinking.

Students should be informed of the purpose of a discussion prior to being assigned material to read in preparation for that discussion. Monitoring an ongoing discussion to ensure that students interact with one another as well as with the teacher is a sound practice. When interaction is strictly between the teacher and the student, with the teacher initiating a series of questions aimed at assessing the student's level of learning, recitation, not discussion, is the result.

Issues related to content area discussion

As a teaching method, recitation has been criticized for its emphasis on a rapid fire question and answer format aimed primarily at ensuring factual or knowledge level learning among students. Despite the criticism, the popularity of the recitation method has shown no sign of abatement over the past sixty years (Stodolsky, Ferguson, & Wimpelberg, 1981).

Recently, however, a series of research reports and recommendations based on several national assessments of reading achievement have suggested the need to redefine the role of discussion in relation to higher level reading skills. Three issues related to content area discussion need to be addressed. One, if the persistence of the recitation method fails to provide the kind of instruction needed to advance students' higher level reading skills, what does the discussion method offer as an alternative? Two, how can the discussion method highlight the importance of the textbook, supplementary texts, tradebooks, newspapers, and other media sources? Three, how can the discussion method support a student centered curriculum and thereby provide a balance to the more teacher directed recitation method?

An alternative to the recitation method

According to the 1984 National Assessment of Educational Progress (NAEP) in reading (see *The Reading Report Card,* 1985), 40 percent of the thirteen year olds and 16 percent of the seventeen year olds still in school had not acquired the intermediate literacy skills necessary for drawing inferences and reaching generalizations about key ideas from content area texts. Even more disturbing was the lack of proficiency among those students in terms of ability to react critically to what they read or to question their interpretations of text in the face of opposing arguments. Such results prompted the authors of *The Reading Report Card* to recommend an increased emphasis on teaching higher level reading skills with specific attention given to discussion as one means of improving those skills.

The textbook as a primary source of information

At issue here is the need to motivate students to use their textbooks and other sources for primary information, rather than rely on their teachers' use of recitation and lecture methods to spoon feed the information to them (Ratekin et al., 1985; Smith & Feathers, 1983a, 1983b). The discussion method, with its emphasis on student talk, offers a means by which teachers can make assignments reflecting the expectation that students (and not the teacher) will develop an understanding of the concepts presented.

This purposeful shifting of responsibility from the teacher to the students would not preclude the necessity of teaching students how to glean important information from their textbooks. Nor would this shift in responsibility preclude the teacher from making the kinds of curricular decisions necessary for meeting schoolwide program objectives.

Discussion and the student centered curriculum

Characteristic of the recitation method is its tendency "to limit spoken language to the teacher telling and the pupil replying to cross examination" (Barnes, 1976, p. 84), as in this fictionalized account of an interaction between Lennie and his teacher in Byars' book, *The TV Kid* (1976, p. 70):

> "Do you think he was just talking about *one* year passing?" the teacher went on.
> "Or do you think, Lennie, that the poet was seeing his whole life as a year, that he was seeing his whole life slipping past?"
> "I'm not sure." Lennie's hand was still on his chin as if ready to stroke a long gray beard.
> "Class?"
> "His whole life slipping past," the class chorused together. They had had this teacher so long that they could tell, just from the way she asked a question, what they were supposed to answer.

If concern is for the "right" answer and lower level skills, then the class in Byars' book has learned its lesson well. However, as evidenced in *Landscapes: A State-of-the-Art Assessment of Reading Comprehension Research, 1974-1984* (Crismore, 1985), there has been a shift in how researchers and practitioners think about comprehension instruction. This shift places greater emphasis on the active involvement of students in the comprehension process and calls for teachers to challenge students to question, rethink, and elaborate on what they have read. According to the authors of *The Reading Report Card* (1985, p.9), "in that process, students will also be acquiring the higher-level reading comprehension skills that so many are presently lacking."

The remaining chapters in this book take account of the three issues, especially focusing on the discussion method as a means of improving students' understanding of their content area reading assignments. By focusing on the discussion method, we do not mean that using it, alone, will lead to improved comprehension. Just as there are several reasons why more students do not currently demonstrate higher level reading skills, there are also several approaches to teaching those skills.

Summary

Discussion is important both as a communication skill and as the foundation for developing higher level reading skills. Although multiple definitions of *discussion* exist, we believe a discussion must satisfy these three criteria: Discussants should put forth multiple points of view and stand ready to change their minds about the matter under discussion; students should interact with one another as well as with the teacher; and the interaction should exceed the typical two or three word phrase units common to recitation lessons. Instructional purposes for using the discussion method include subject mastery, attitude change (issue oriented), and problem solving. In contrast, recitations primarily serve this instructional objective: rapid fire questioning and answering with an orientation toward factual or knowledge level learning. Although the recitation method has remained popular through the years, information from recent research and school reform movement reports suggests the need to promote the use of discussion. Specifically, the discussion method should be considered an alternative to recitation; the textbook needs to figure more prominently in content area discussions; and greater emphasis should be placed on actively involving students in postreading discussions.

References

Alvermann, D.E., O'Brien, D.G., Dillon, D.R., and Smith, L.C. *Textbook reading assignments: An analysis of teacher-student discussions.* Paper presented at the Conference on Reading Research, CORR-5, Atlanta, Georgia, May 1984.

Barnes, D. *From communication to curriculum.* Harmondsworth, Middlesex, England: Penguin Books, 1976.

Bloom, B.S. The thought process of students in discussion. In S.J. French (Ed.), *Accent on teaching.* New York: Harper & Brothers, 1954, 23-46.

Bridges, D. *Education, democracy, and discussion.* Windsor, England: NFER Publishing, 1979.

Byars, B. *The TV kid.* New York: Viking Press, 1976.

Corson, D. Oral language in the middle school. *Middle School Journal,* 1984, *1,* 30-31, 35.

Crismore, A. (Ed.). *Landscapes: A state-of-the-art assessment of reading comprehension research, 1974-1984.* Contract No. 300-83-0130. Washington, DC: U.S. Department of Education, 1985.

Dillon, J.T. Duration of response to teacher questions and statements. *Contemporary Educational Psychology,* 1981, *6,* 1-11.

Dillon, J.T. Research on questioning and discussion. *Educational Leadership,* 1984, *42,* 50-56.

Gall, M.D., and Gall, J.P. The discussion method. In N.L. Gage (Ed.), *Psychology of teaching methods.* National Society for the Study of Education, Seventy-Fifth Yearbook, Part 1. Chicago: University of Chicago Press, 1976, 166-216.

Landon, J. *The principles and practices of teaching and class management.* London: Edinburgh University Press, 1899.

National Assessment of Educational Progress. *The reading report card.* Princeton, NJ: Educational Testing Service, 1985.

Ratekin, N., Simpson, M.L., Alvermann, D.E., and Dishner, E.K. Why teachers resist content reading instruction. *Journal of Reading,* 1985, *28,* 432-437.

Smith, F.R., and Feathers, K.M. Teacher and student perceptions of content area reading. *Journal of Reading,* 1983a, *6,* 348-354.

Smith, F.R., and Feathers, K.M. The role of reading in content classrooms: Assumption vs. reality. *Journal of Reading,* 1983b, *27,* 262-267.

Stanford, G., and Stanford, B.D. *Learning discussion skills through games.* New York: Citation Press, 1969.

Stodolsky, S.S., Ferguson, T.L., and Wimpelberg, K. The recitation persists, but what does it look like? *Journal of Curriculum Studies,* 1981, *13,* 121-130.

2

The role of discussion in promoting reading comprehension

T he purpose of this chapter is to establish that discussion plays an important role in helping students understand their content area reading assignments. First, discussion is described as an integral part of comprehension instruction. Next, classroom conditions thought to foster text based content area discussions are examined. Finally, several student centered alternatives to teacher questioning are explored.

Discussion:
An integral part of comprehension instruction

Reasons vary for believing that discussion plays an important role in helping students comprehend content area reading assignments. Some educators believe that the ability to enrich and refine knowledge gained from reading text depends on opportunities for hearing the information discussed from others' points of view. Meanings shared in discussion groups are not merely a collection of individual meanings; they are part of new sets of meanings developed as members talk and listen to one another (Pinnell, 1984).

Recitation and the lecture method cannot compete with discussion in offering opportunities for students to communicate their views to other students with different views. In traditional recitation and lecture formats, teachers are seen as authority figures whose academic credentials tend to inhibit rather than foster students' active shaping of knowledge gained from reading. Teachers who use discussion create a learning opportunity that encourages students to enrich and refine the understandings they have derived from reading their assigned texts (Bridges, 1985).

Enriched understanding

Discussion can enrich students' understanding by causing them to view learned facts in light of others' interpretations of those facts. Discussion also can reinforce long term memory. Students who articulate their ideas about a concept to others have a good chance of later recalling information related to that concept.

Refined understanding

Discussion can help students refine their understanding of what they have read, particularly in classrooms where there is concern for clarity and precision in verbal expression. This concern frequently leads to an expansion of specialized vocabularies within the various content areas. Another way teachers can use discussion to refine comprehension is to require students to give reasons in support of, or in argument against, contradictory opinions that arise. Finally, understanding is refined when students eliminate logical inconsistencies and contradictions in their own thinking as they read and simultaneously monitor their comprehension.

Text based discussion

Using text based discussions to increase students' reliance on a variety of print sources can put students in control of their own learning. Discussion gives students the opportunity to analyze orally an author's intended meaning in the company of their peers. A text based discussion makes it safe for students to disagree, to put forth alternative hypotheses, and to test those hypotheses in light of their peers' responses.

Text based discussions offer numerous opportunities for teachers to foster students' critical thinking. For example, through class discussion, teachers can demonstrate the importance of evaluating texts for accuracy, for possible biases, and for assumptions made by authors. By listening to students talk, teachers can determine if there is a concern for developing understanding among the discussants. For instance, do the students exhibit an interest in enriching and refining one another's understanding of the topic?

Text based discussions help alleviate the feeling of isolation students experience when they interact only with the text. When reading is viewed as a natural part of the social structure of the classroom, students enjoy interacting with one another. Reading for social purposes at middle school and beyond is easier when teachers are separated from the situation (Bloome & Green, 1985). This distancing of the authority figure ensures that students will have to rely on themselves as interpreters of what they read.

Another technique for boosting students' self-reliance involves teacher assigned related readings. By encouraging students to use their textbooks as springboards to other printed sources (tradebooks, news magazines, original documents), teachers can create an environment for discussion in which comparing and contrasting sources, noting points of view, and determining a writer's purpose are commonplace activities among the discussants.

Student centered alternatives to teacher questioning

One of the simplest things teachers can do to limit the amount of teacher talk and increase the amount of student talk during a discussion is to stop asking questions. Dillon's (1984) seven alternatives to questioning provide teachers with a means of actively involving students in postreading discussions. Illustrations of these alternatives follow.

Setting   *For homework, Mr. Noonan's tenth grade world history class had read a section in their text on the establishment of Fascism in Europe prior to the start of World War II. As the class opens, Noonan is conducting a review of the events leading to the Nazi takeover.*

Noonan
From the start, the Weimar Republic was faced with insurmountable problems.

Alternative 1.   Make a declarative or factual statement. Noonan used a statement, rather than a question, to get the discussion going. He then waited for students to elaborate on the statement.

Noonan (later, to Danita)
From your point of view, then, runaway inflation was the worst problem Germany faced at the time Hitler began his rise to power.

Alternative 2.   Make a reflective statement. By reflecting on what Danita had said, Noonan showed that he had listened to her and had found her contribution worthwhile. Note that he did not attempt to probe more deeply with a question such as, "What do you mean by runaway inflation?" However, another student did take up the inflation issue.

Noonan (still later in the discussion)
Pete, your strong feeling about the Nazi persecution of the Jews seems to have influenced your evaluation of Hitler's well known autobiography.

Alternative 3.   Describe the student's state of mind. The intent of Noonan's statement was to invite Pete to analyze the reason for his intense dislike of *Mein*

Kampf. It was also an invitation to others to challenge Pete's evaluation of the book.

Noonan (when no one took up the challenge)
It would be helpful if we knew some of the criteria Pete used in evaluating the book.

Alternative 4. Invite student to elaborate on a statement. Instead of asking, "Pete, why do you think as you do?" Noonan gave Pete an "out" in the event that he didn't want to elaborate further. At the same time, Noonan's statement opened the floor to other speakers who might care to hypothesize about the criteria Pete used.

Noonan (later, to Violet)
You need to ask me why I referred to the Aryans as the "master race."

Alternative 5. Encourage the student to ask a question. Noonan frequently employed this alternative when he felt that the students did not attribute enough importance to something he had said or when they had overlooked an important concept in the text.

Noonan (rather matter of factly)
Jesse Owens won four gold medals, but Hitler was correct in saying that Owens was "less than human."

Alternative 6. Encourage students to ask questions of one another. One way to encourage student to student interaction is to make a controversial statement and then back out of the crossfire that inevitably erupts. In this instance, one student, Beth, asked the boy sitting across the aisle, "Who is Jesse Owens?" Noonan's controversial statement also sparked some give and take between two students who enjoyed playing the devil's advocate.

Noonan (Following the boisterous discussion about Hitler's attitude toward blacks, Noonan said nothing.)
Alternative 7. Maintain a deliberate silence. This technique signals a change in pace. Maintaining a deliberate silence is an appropriate way of encouraging reflectivity among the discussants. It is especially good to use after a student has shared a rather profound insight (appreciative silence). To be noticeable, a deliberate silence must last three seconds or longer.

In addition to substituting statements for questions, teachers interested in more student centered discussions should make a conscious effort to avoid reacting to every response a student makes. Once implemented, this simple technique helps to keep a discussion from ping ponging between the teacher and individual students. It also helps to increase the amount of time given to discussion among students (Klinzing-Eurich & Klinzing, 1985).

Summary

The three major issues that evolved from redefining the role of discussion in relation to comprehending content area texts (see Chapter 1) serve as the framework for the information in this chapter. Discussion is an integral part of the comprehension process. We encourage teachers to use text based discussion as a means of shifting the responsibility for learning from the teacher to the student, and we present ideas for actively involving students in postreading discussions.

References

Bloome, D., and Green, J. Looking at reading instruction: Sociolinguistic and ethnographic approaches. In C.N. Hedley and A.N. Baratta (Eds.), *Contexts of reading.* Norwood, NJ: Ablex, 1985, 167-184.

Bridges, D. *Education, democracy, and discussion.* Windsor, England: NFER Publishing, 1979.

Bridges, D. *Quality of understanding in classroom discussion.* Paper presented at the annual meeting of the American Educational Research Association, Chicago, April 1985.

Dillon, J.T. Research on questioning and discussion. *Educational Leadership,* 1984, *42,* 50-56.

Klinzing-Eurich, G., and Klinzing, H.G. *Teacher questions, student utterances, and teacher reactions in classroom discussions.* Paper presented at the annual meeting of the American Educational Research Association, Chicago, April 1985.

Pinnell, G.S. Communication in small group settings. *Theory into Practice,* 1984, *23,* 246-254.

3
The influence of context on discussion practices

C hapter 3 begins with a brief description of the context for classroom discussion and what it takes to be successful in that context. Following that is a more comprehensive look at three factors of classroom contexts that influence discussion practices: teacher talk, the textbook, and physical space.

In teaching reading, the term *context* is used to refer to information in written text that explains the meanings of individual words—hence, the frequently heard phrase, using context clues to unlock word meanings. Sometimes researchers refer to science classrooms as having contexts different from the contexts of social studies classrooms. Unfortunately, this oversimplification of context may lead to the incorrect conclusion that one classroom context differs from another purely on the basis of the content taught. Although different content areas do place some constraints on the types of activities involved in teaching the subject matter, the differences are usually minor.

Context includes all of the factors that affect classroom events. In a sense, the context is a picture that includes the foreground and background of an event. In this instance, the event is classroom discussion, and the context includes the immediately perceivable as well as the underlying factors affecting that event.

Context for classroom discussion

Contextual factors that affect classroom discussion include the stated instructional objectives, the physical setting, and the format of the discussion (e.g., whole class versus small group). The context for classroom discussion includes more subtle factors as well. Classroom discussion may change rapidly depending on the discussants' individual perspectives and expectations, their interpersonal relationships with other discussants, and their mutually held expectations as members of a common group. Individuals who are effective in classroom discussion know how to "read the context" as well as how to "predict the context and shape it so their comments will fit in and be understood" (Pinnell, 1984, p. 247).

Some students are more adept than others at reading and shaping the context. For example, contrast Neil's performance with the performance of his seventh grade peers in the following discussion of Kurt Vonnegut's short story "Harrison Bergeron" (1975).

Setting *The discussion opens with Neil's attempt to rationalize why Harrison Bergeron, the main character in the story, has proclaimed himself Emperor and has resorted to the use of violence to rid the people of the dreaded handicappers (mind jangling earphones inserted into the ears of intelligent individuals to make them just average, like everyone else). Roberto had asked why Harrison used violence when the story said he was intelligent.*

Neil
Well, I think he went about it so he can prove that he is an Emperor. 'Cause he, if he can show everybody he's Emperor, then he *is* Emperor. Then he can use his intelligence to straighten out the world.

Teacher
How does the author tell you that?

Neil
Well, um. (teacher waited at least 10 seconds)

Teacher
Help him.

Shana
In the book on page 6, it says, um, " 'Even as I stand here' he bellowed, 'crippled, hobbled, sickened, I am a greater ruler than any man who ever lived! Now watch me become what I can become!' " You know, he was, um, trying to become Emperor because he thought that he could be Emperor, and he thought that he could be a greater ruler than any man that ever lived.

Katherine
By what Shana says, it sounds like he really does want to be different. He doesn't want to be like everybody else. He wants to make his fortune and make his life for himself and not let other people make it for him.

Teacher
Roberto, have we resolved your question? (This is in reference to a question posed earlier by Roberto, the one Neil attempted to answer.)

Roberto
Yeah.

Teacher

To your satisfaction?

Roberto

Yeah, I think so. I've also discovered that well, these people needed an Emperor, someone to lead them because they had no one to lead them after those handicappers were destroyed. They had no government; they would be totally lost. And they would elect the same people who had put them in this place.

Neil

Then they might as well go back to the 1770s.

Teacher

So you are saying that they needed someone like this to take over. Is there anything more to be said on this subject?

Paul

Yeah, I think he also wanted everybody else to be as much as they could be. I think that's probably why he got mad at those two musicians, because he knew somehow, he knew they could be better. He wanted them to do their best.

Neil

He wanted everybody to do the same thing as him...(teacher interrupts Neil)

Teacher

Susan, did you want to say something? (Susan had raised her hand)

Susan

It was about, um, it was about Roberto's question. Well, Harrison might have used violence because the story says a lot of people have handicap things in their ears, and you know they would go off, and they'd mix up all their thoughts. When Harrison got his handicappers off, he was intelligent but nobody else was, so they couldn't understand his intelligent remarks.

Teacher

All right. Have we resolved that question to everyone's satisfaction?

Roberto

I have a new question.

An analysis of the context for the discussion is a study of contrasts in how students gain the floor. The teacher calls on Shana to help when it becomes clear Neil cannot respond to the teacher's question, "How does the author tell you that?" Later, the teacher calls on Susan in response to her raised hand. However, for Katherine and Paul, waiting to be recognized by the teacher is not a prerequisite for turntaking; they are self-initiators. But when Neil attempts to initiate a response to Roberto's comment, the teacher chooses to ignore Neil in favor of following up on Roberto's line of reasoning. Ten lines later, the teacher interrupts Neil to call on another student.

Alvermann, Dillon, O'Brien

At first glance it appears that either Neil was not a good reader or the teacher had low expectations of his ability to contribute anything of worth to the discussion. Based on a personal interview with Neil's teacher, the latter seems likely. The teacher said that Neil had been placed in her class by mistake. According to her, Neil was not capable of keeping up with other students. Ms. Watts had requested that Neil be transferred to another class section. What it took to be successful in this particular teacher's discussion group was beyond Neil's control. No matter how hard he tried to predict the context of the discussion, he was unsuccessful.

Roberto, on the other hand, was successful both in reading and in shaping the context. His knack for asking thought provoking questions caught the teacher's attention, so she was careful to ask Roberto if the group had resolved his question to his satisfaction. By volunteering "I have a new question," Roberto effectively assured himself of a dominant role in the next round of talk. Watts could curb Roberto's attempt to dominate the discussion; however, if past performance is any indication, it is unlikely she would do so.

Contextual factors that affect discussion practices

Studies show that students are taught to depend on the teacher, not the text, as their primary source of information (Ratekin et al., 1985; Smith & Feathers, 1983a, 1983b). Reasons for this dependency are thought to stem from students' perceptions that it is easier to understand the teacher than the textbook. Teachers enjoy four distinct advantages over textbooks: teachers can tailor information to a student's level of understanding, teachers know the appropriate background knowledge to tap when new or difficult concepts are encountered, teachers can focus attention on only the relevant parts of a body of explanatory material, and teachers have many different ways of monitoring a student's comprehension (Schallert & Kleiman, 1979).

For these reasons students are often inclined to place a teacher in the role of lecturer-discussant and, thus, abdicate their responsibility for taking an active role in class discussions.

Teacher talk

In a monograph entitled *Teacher Talk: Language in the Classroom* (1978, p. 18), Heath addresses the issue of why it is beneficial to examine the nature of teacher talk *with* and *among* teachers:

Alternatives to unconscious use of teacher talk can come only when teachers are made aware of the structural and functional features of their own language. The goal of change is not only for teachers to shift from a role of direct influence to an indirect one, but to provide them with imaginative alternatives to many of the strategies and routines of classroom [sic] that have become fossilized and make teaching and learning boring for everyone concerned.

The degree to which teacher talk can dominate a class discussion is evident from the transcribed segments of a videotaped discussion in Mr. Morton's room.

Setting *As the discussion opens, the teacher reminds the students that they are continuing in the previously assigned chapter on earth chemistry.*

Morton
As we have had an opportunity to read further in our textbook chapter, we find the authors writing about the origin of the earth. The text brought up two terms that are familiar to us—*hypothesis* and *theory.* (long pause)

Morton
What is a hypothesis? Joe? (Joe was talking)

Joe
It's an educated guess.

Morton
An educated guess is a hypothesis. What did I ask?

Joe
What is a hypothesis?

Morton
Okay. You said an educated guess. I always get that "educated guess" answer. What does that *mean*?

Joe (almost inaudible)
Hypothesis.

Morton
All right. (accepting tone of voice) Do you want to answer or do you want someone else to answer the question? (said with patience)

Joe
Somebody else. (with no visible sign of anxiety or embarrassment)

Morton
Okay. Kenny.

Kenny
It's um, facts you have brought together to make one statement, like trying to prove the hypothesis you made is right. Like drawing a diagram of actual...(voice trails off and teacher interrupts)

Alvermann, Dillon, O'Brien

Morton

Jerome.

Jerome

It could be true.

Morton

It could be true. It's something you feel. You have enough factual information to make you think it's something you could find out about....Isn't it a type of guess based on evidence you already have? It's kind of like an answer you hope to find. Right? A few days ago we were making some hypotheses, right?

Several students (in unison)

Uh huh.

Morton

And we were saying things like, "Is there a relationship between weight and height?" and some people said, "Sure, the taller you are the more you weigh." That was our hypothesis: as height increases, weight increases. That's something we believe to be the truth. Okay, and then we would perform an experiment and find out. What about theory? How does theory differ from that? Ah, LeeAnn?

LeeAnn

It's supported by more information.

Morton

Okay.

Shawn

It can be proven. (thoughtfully)

Morton

It can be proven. Can it? There are some theories about the origin of the earth. Do you suppose we can ever prove them? There are some that have stood the test of time – so far.

Kenny

So far.

Morton

Yes.

Tejas

It doesn't have to be true.

Morton

One day it could be proven not to be true, right? Sometimes theories will stay around for the longest time....Remember earlier in the year we talked about the theory that the earth was the center of the solar system? That theory stood the test of time until Copernicus....Okay, but a theory...you've got more with it, right? A theory is a scientific explanation and a hypothesis is something you hold to be true. Okay. I also asked you to read about the earth's matter....(The discussion takes a new turn.)

Influence of Context on Discussion Practices

Initially, Morton seemed interested in drawing out students' definitions of *hypothesis*. He stayed with Joe through several attempts, but later gave up and told Joe the definition ("Isn't it a type of guess based on evidence you already have?"). Morton behaved similarly when he asked LeeAnn to define *theory*. Each time he incorrectly assumed that the terms were familiar to the students (cf., Morton's introductory comment "The text brought up two terms that are familiar to us—*hypothesis* and *theory*"). Most of the students were not familiar enough with the terms to participate in the discussion, so Morton did most of the talking.

Rather than assume that his students would be able to produce definitions for the two words in question, Morton might have asked them to merely recognize the differences in meaning between the two terms. For example, he might have written two statements on the chalkboard, one that dealt with Copernicus' theory of the relation of the planets to the sun and one that dealt with the hypothesis that UFOS carry individuals with advanced intelligence. Morton might have asked students to identify which statement reflected a theory and which reflected a hypothesis. He also might have asked students to give reasons for their choices. This type of activity would tend to foster more student talk relative to teacher talk.

The role of the textbook

Thinking of reading at the secondary school level usually brings images of readers interacting with books or other written material. Typically, discussion is not part of the schema for secondary school reading assignments. In fact, for most students, reading is more private than social. Consider this hypothetical assignment: "Okay, everybody read Chapter 16 for tomorrow. There will be an exam with some questions from that chapter." You can picture students carting their textbooks home and engaging in private struggles with Chapter 16. Once students leave the traditional "reading group" (most often associated with basal reading instruction), they are expected to learn the material on their own.

There is an alternative to isolated reading of textbook assignments. What would happen if the textbook were used as an active element in classroom discussion? What if reading were treated as an event during class time rather than as an outside activity? What if interaction with a textbook involved several class members working together in a group?

There are viable ways for using the textbook in a discussion. When viewed as an integral part of the classroom discussion process, a textbook can serve a variety of functions: as a source of factual information, as a jumping off point for a debate, or as a resource for critical reading activities. For example, when discussion is used as an outlet for examining what students learned from applying their critical reading skills to a particular content assignment, teachers should provide students with a set of discussion guidelines that speak directly to them as critical readers. *The Bill of Rights and Responsibilities of Critical Readers* (Mangieri & Baldwin, 1978) is one such set of guidelines. Under the responsibilities are some parameters of critical reading that students can use in structuring information they want to discuss from their assigned reading material. Under the rights are some acceptable discussion behaviors.

The Bill of Rights and Responsibilities of Critical Readers

Responsibilities

1. You have the responsibility of getting all of the facts, and getting them straight.

2. You are responsible for separating verifiable facts from opinion when you read.

3. You are responsible for resisting fallacious lines of reasoning and propaganda.

4. You are responsible for deciding what is relevant and irrelevant when you read.

5. You have the responsibility to entertain the author's point of view objectively. Negativism and criticism are not the same thing.

6. For better or worse, you are responsible for the conclusions you draw when reading, even if the author provides you with false or misleading information.

Rights

1. You have a right to all the facts, though you may have to root them out for yourself.

2. You have the right to be exposed to contrasting points of view.

3. You have the right to ask questions, even though it annoys the teacher.

4. You have the right to your own opinion, even if it contradicts recognized authority.

Up to this point, the focus has been on contexts for classroom discussion that are primarily defined by verbal interaction. However, another important, though often neglected, contextual factor that can affect what happens during a discussion is physical space.

Control of physical space

The definition and control of physical space in the classroom deserve scrutiny. How is available space used? Where are the students in relation to the teacher? How does proximity affect the types of discussion that occur?

The way classroom space is used indicates how teachers want students to view teachers' roles in discussions. Teachers who wish to be considered authoritarian may choose to stand in the front of the room at some stationary post. Teachers may use physical distance as a classroom management technique. However, the organization of physical space for optimal classroom management may create a setting that inhibits an open forum for discussion. For example, seating by rows rather than in circles may offer the teacher better class control, but it may also decrease the likelihood of a good discussion in which a free exchange of ideas is encouraged by virtue of seeing the audience. The horseshoe is a good compromise between row and circle arrangements. The horseshoe arrangement permits discussants to see one another and to communicate face to face. At the same time, positioning the teacher at the open end of the horseshoe creates physical distance and has implications for class control.

Some forms of small group seating arrangements have been observed to foster active student participation in discussions. For instance, groups of five students may be seated at round tables in a semicircle around the teacher's desk. Rooms in which eight foot rectangular tables are the norm typically have a small group of students working at either end with empty table space between. In some discussion formats, grouping may not be a good idea, especially if students tend to interact more with their peers than with their teachers or textbooks. Table seating arrangements are most conducive to group interaction when the purpose for discussion is either to change attitudes (issue oriented discussion) or to engage students in some form of problem solving task. When subject mastery is the purpose for discussion and the teacher plans to mix lecture with discussion, students may be seated on opposite sides of the room facing one another. When the teacher comes to the part of the lesson that requires students to be in several small groups, students move their chairs into the small group configuration.

Where students sit in relation to the teacher and to one another influences participation in classroom discussion. For example, research on discussion practices (Gall & Gall, 1976) revealed that students who sat in the center rows, toward the front, facing the teacher participated more than students who sat toward the rear or on the sides of the room. The research also showed that more talkative individuals should be seated opposite quieter ones. However, individuals who monopolize discussions should be seated next to one another.

Summary

Metaphorically speaking, context is a picture that includes the foreground and background of an event. Applied to discussion, the context includes the immediately perceivable as well as the more subtle factors affecting that event. To be a successful participant in a classroom discussion, an individual must know how to read the context and how to predict and shape it. Three contextual factors that influence discussion practices are teacher talk, the textbook, and physical space. Each of these factors was described in this chapter.

References

Gall, M.D., and Gall, J.P. The discussion method. In N.L. Gage (Ed.), *Psychology of teaching methods*. National Society for the Study of Education, Seventy-Fifth Yearbook, Part 1. Chicago: University of Chicago Press, 1976, 166-216.

Heath, S.B. *Teacher-talk: Language in the classroom*. Language in Education: Theory and Practice Report No. 9. Arlington, VA: Center for Applied Linguistics, 1978.

Mangieri, J., and Baldwin, R.S. *Effective reading techniques: Business and personal applications*. San Francisco, CA: Canfield Press, 1978.

Pinnell, G.S. Communication in small group settings. *Theory into Practice*, 1984, *23*, 246-254.

Ratekin, N., Simpson, M., Alvermann, D., and Dishner, E. Why teachers resist content reading instruction. *Journal of Reading*, 1985, *28*, 432-437.

Schallert, D.L., and Kleiman, G.M. *Some reasons why teachers are easier to understand than textbooks*. 1979. (ED 172 189)

Smith, F.R., and Feathers, K.M. Teacher and student perceptions of content area reading. *Journal of Reading*, 1983a, *26*, 348-354.

Smith, F.R., and Feathers, K.M. The role of reading in content classrooms: Assumption vs. reality. *Journal of Reading*, 1983b, *27*, 262-267.

Vonnegut, Kurt, Jr. Harrison Bergeron. In R.P. Dennis and E.P. Moldof (Eds.), *Junior great books*. Chicago: Great Books Foundation, 1975, 1-8.

4

Planning the discussion

T his chapter highlights the importance of planning to successful classroom discussions. Teaching with the discussion method assumes a
basic knowledge of how to plan; that is, how to specify the purposes or
objectives of a discussion, select appropriate content, select appropriate
strategies, organize for whole class or small group instruction, and evaluate the success of the discussion. These five aspects of planning a discussion may overlap and become almost automatic, but for purposes of
illustration and analysis, each is treated separately here.

Specifying the purposes or objectives

In addition to the three broad instructional purposes of discussion (mastering the content, debating an issue, solving a problem), teachers may have
specific objectives in mind when they plan a discussion. McKeachie (1978)
has listed a number of such objectives:

- to tap the resources students bring to their school subjects;
- to provide students with the time necessary to formulate their own
  applications of abstract principles;
- to obtain immediate feedback on how well students are understanding the lesson content;
- to provide students with instruction and practice in how to think
  about particular subject matter;
- to build students' confidence in their ability to evaluate the logic of
  their own ideas and the ideas of others;
- to promote student awareness of the need to formulate problems and
  questions based on information gained from reading or listening to
  a lecture; and
- to foster the notion that new ideas may challenge and sometimes
  change previous ideas.

An overriding objective of most teacher planned discussions is the facilitation of learning through increased student motivation. The motivational properties of the discussion method are thought to include the desirability of communicating with peers and the need to have one's ideas heard and accepted by others. Known research suggests that secondary school students value discussion highly. National Merit Scholarship winners reported that teachers who allowed time for classroom discussion contributed most to students' desire to learn (McKeachie, 1978). In addition, the results of a study (Schallert & Tierney, 1982) funded by the National Institute of Education revealed that high school students perceive classroom discussion as valuable in helping them understand reading assignments. In that study, students in biology and history classes completed a survey in which they were asked what teachers could do to make textbooks more comprehensible. Over 75 percent of the students agreed that teachers could give them time in class to discuss ideas in their textbooks.

Selecting appropriate content

Analyzing portions of a textbook chapter to identify the content appropriate for the purposes or objectives of the discussion is the second step in the planning process. When learning that new ideas sometimes change previous ideas is the objective, a teacher would look for the text segment containing the greatest number of counterintuitive ideas. For instance, a physics teacher might skim a chapter on Newton's laws of motion to find the text segment that describes what trajectory a horizontally launched object would take. If the teacher thought students were likely to hold fast to the impetus theory (the commonly mistaken belief that an object maintains its trajectory because of an inner force acquired when the object was set in motion), he or she might plan in advance of the discussion to demonstrate one of Newton's laws of motion.

When the purpose of a discussion is issue oriented, a different approach is needed when selecting appropriate content. For instance, a social studies teacher might select the text segment that has a photograph of women correspondents at the front line in Vietnam during the height of the military offensive. The teacher might open the discussion by asking students to speculate on the photographer's intent or motive in taking the photograph (Rudduck, 1979).

Selecting appropriate content for a problem solving discussion involves another set of criteria. One way teachers can ensure that students will be committed to solving the problem is to involve them in its selection.

This can be accomplished by providing students with opportunities to speak openly of their interests and concerns, and then linking them in some logical way to the content of the text.

Although specifying the purposes and objectives of a discussion preceded the section on selecting appropriate content, the planning process is not necessarily a linear one. Sometimes the nature of the content will determine which discussion purpose a teacher chooses. It is important that neither specifying objectives nor selecting appropriate content should be overlooked in the rush to get to the most popular aspect of planning – strategy selection.

Selecting appropriate strategies

Deciding which strategies to use with particular purposes and objectives is an activity that consumes little time once teachers have their favorite repertoire of strategies. The guidelines for selecting strategies that follow include suggestions for accommodating individual differences within the various types of discussion.

Subject mastery discussions

Traditionally, teachers have focused students' attention on pre and postreading questions to help them acquire the essential information for a discussion of the assigned content material. Several alternative strategies capitalize on the integration of oral and written language. Hill's method of discussion (1977) is well suited to subject mastery discussions in which students are accountable for the recall of factual level information and for the definitions of vocabulary terms.

Manzo and Casale's (1985) Listen-Read-Discuss Strategy (see Chapter 5 in this book) is well suited to students who depend on teachers' lectures to aid their understanding and retention of the content. Similarly, Davidson's (1982) discussion mapping strategy holds promise for students who read their assignments but do not retain the information long enough to discuss it.

Probing is an important strategy for subject mastery discussions. Teachers need a number of probes they can use to encourage students to go beyond their initial, sometimes superficial, responses. The following list of probes includes examples drawn from a seventh grade social studies class discussion on the events leading up to the Civil War (Alvermann et al., 1985).

Alvermann, Dillon, O'Brien

Probes that sought to *clarify*.

Teacher
All right, I know *Uncle Tom's Cabin* was a book, but why was it so important?

Steve
It was a book written by Harriet Beecher Stowe, and it was um…about slaves.

Teacher
It was factual, I assume?

Steve
The Southerners thought it was exaggerated. The Northerners were upset, too. I guess it was fiction.

Probe that sought to have the student *justify* his response.

Teacher
What evidence is there in your textbook that makes you think *Uncle Tom's Cabin* was fiction?

Steve
It [the textbook] says "it offered readers a fictional account of how life was on a Southern plantation."

Probe that *refocused* the student's attention on the key concept.

Teacher
So if the book was only fictional, why was it so important?

Betty
It, um, the uneasy calm between the North and South was broken. That was the end of the calmness between them.

Probes that *prompted*.

Teacher
What might Harriet Beecher Stowe have been trying to tell the world back then?

Betty
I'm not sure….

Teacher
How did she describe the life of the slaves?

Betty
She said the slaves were being sold and separated and were being beaten and forced to do backbreakin' work.

Probe that fostered *greater student to student interaction*.

Teacher
Okay, would each of you turn to your neighbor on either side of the aisle and ask one another "Why does the teacher think *Uncle Tom's Cabin* was so important?"

Planning for subject mastery discussions entails making plans for responding to individual differences in student participation level. Contrary to popular belief, students who elect not to talk during a discussion learn on an equal par with their more vocal peers. Perhaps it is the covert learning responses evoked by the teacher's questions that are critical to learning and not the students' responses (Gall & Gall, 1976). Although verbal participation in a subject mastery discussion may not be necessary for the discussion to be effective, teachers generally look for signs that students are motivated and able to comprehend their assignments. A student's willingness to discuss previously assigned material is one of those signs. When such signs are missing, some teachers plan a written assignment that students can choose as an option to participating in a discussion.

Issue oriented discussions

Choices of compatible strategies for use with issue oriented discussions are not as plentiful as they are for subject mastery discussions. Guidelines for planning an issue oriented discussion involve identifying a controversial topic. Typically, controversial issues come from perceived or real threats to self, a cherished belief, or an economic interest. It is crucial that students view the issue as being important. One way to ensure this is to involve students in the selection process with the teacher's guidance. For example, if teachers know a particular issue will require students to consult information sources not readily available, they may suggest that students look into a different issue.

Planning ways to prepare students for an issue oriented discussion is time well spent. One guideline involves obtaining material (evidence) that will help to initiate the discussion and to "feed" it once it is underway. For example, in planning a discussion on the new town ordinance that banned sidewalk cafés, one teacher chose letters to the editor and pictorial material from a local newspaper to supplement the textbook's treatment of city ordinances.

A second useful guideline for an issue oriented discussion involves finding ways to promote understanding and empathy for individuals who take stands on the issue. Otherwise, the discussion can turn into a heated, irrational dispute. When individual differences are not taken into account, unthoughtful statements can bring unnecessary grief to some individuals.

Problem solving discussions

Suggested guidelines for facilitating a problem solving discussion derive primarily from Maier's (1963) method (described and illustrated in

Chapter 5 of this book). Briefly, Maier believes that problems should be identified by teachers working in cooperation with students and that problems should grow out of a textbook assignment, a teacher's lecture, students' previous discussions, or a combination of any of these. Maier contends that discussants should be allowed to break the problem into parts and then work in small groups on the same problem part at the same time. This strategy is thought to facilitate a sense of direction in the discussion process. As students work through each of several problem parts, they formulate hypotheses, further clarify the overall problem, obtain additional data, and evaluate various proposed solutions.

This concurrent problem solving process implies a division of labor that has implications for teacher planning. Teachers will need to make decisions about grouping and discussion formats. Will students work with partners within small groups to solve various parts of the problem? Or will members of the small groups function as a whole and appoint one of their members to present their proposed solution to the larger group? Teachers' knowledge of individual differences among students in their classes will guide the decision of how groups should be structured.

A variety of discussion formats exist. Roundtable discussions call for a small group of students and a moderator. Members may discuss their approach to solving the problem in front of the larger group, as in the "fishbowl" technique. Roundtable discussions are particularly effective when diverse solutions are posed by the various small groups. Symposia and panel discussions also lend themselves to problem solving. After all of the small group presentations have been made, panelists or symposia participants may be asked to respond to the various solutions proposed by the small groups. Questions from the "audience" also may be directed to the panelists. Role playing dialogues are especially motivating for the less academically inclined students. This discussion format encourages students to go beyond reading and enact the problem. As the role playing dialogue unfolds, problem solving is viewed.

Organizing for whole class or small group instruction

Simply providing students with an opportunity to talk is not sufficient for effective discussions. Discussion planning must take into account group size and the instructional purpose of the discussion. Although subject mastery and issue oriented discussions are appropriate for both large and small group instruction, teachers derive their own set of rules for matching a particular type of discussion with a particular grouping scheme.

Research on group size in relation to discussion effectiveness is equivocal. The discussion method has been described as being effective with groups of two to twenty students (Gage & Berliner, 1975). A workable group size for most teachers appears to be what they have become accustomed to managing. Consequently, group organization is a more fruitful planning criterion than is group size. What factors determine the effectiveness of the discussion method in large group and small group instruction? Are there particular teacher roles that lend themselves better to one form of group organization than another?

Large group discussion

Content area teachers planning a large group discussion need knowledge of the diversity in their students' beliefs and value structures. An issue oriented discussion among a group of students with a variety of beliefs on a particular issue will be more spirited than the same discussion held among a homogeneously grouped student body. In fact, if there is little diversity in students' beliefs, the issue oriented discussion may fall flat.

When teachers plan large group discussions they need to consider their students' attitudes toward the discussion method. Do students value discussion as a method of learning a particular body of content? If students' previous experiences with discussion have been negative in terms of what they have learned, teachers may want to work on improving group attitudes toward discussion before using it as a means of conveying information.

Small group discussion

Planning for small group discussion entails several decisions. First, it is important to decide on a grouping scheme that fits the instructional purpose for holding the discussion and meets one or more of the specific objectives listed at the beginning of this chapter. The second decision involves the "least group size" principle. In essence, this principle holds that a group should consist of no more individuals than are necessary for completing the assigned task. The research supporting this principle shows that as group size increases, the percentage of members who participate decreases (Gall & Gall, 1976). The third decision is whether to form heterogeneous or homogeneous groups of students. In this regard, the same reasoning holds for small group discussion as for large group discussion.

Alvermann, Dillon, O'Brien

Teacher roles in classroom discussion

Although teachers seldom assume one role to the exclusion of all others, preferring instead to move in and out of several different roles in the course of a discussion, the four roles described are treated as discrete entities for ease of reporting.

The *instructor* role, as its name implies, places teachers in a telling or clarifying position. When overused, this role can result in a discussion that more nearly resembles a lecture and frequently may confuse students, especially if they have been encouraged to assume more active roles in discussion. If students sense that teachers will contribute during silences, they won't take seriously their own responsibilities as discussants. The instructor role works equally well in large or small group discussions.

The *participant* role allows a teacher to assume group membership status. In this role, teachers may contribute to group discussions by sharing information and freely expressing their own opinions. Teachers can guide students to greater independence in learning by modeling different ways of responding and reacting to issues, commenting on others' points of view, and applying critical reading strategies to difficult concepts in the textbooks. Care must be taken in using the participant role, however. Teachers' ideas and comments tend to be viewed as more credible than students' contributions. Also, teachers' ideas may be seen as less open to questions and constructive criticism.

The *consultant* or counselor role places a teacher in the position of serving as an advisor. A teacher must be willing and able to direct students toward finding answers on their own. The consultant role works especially well when students are divided into small groups; teachers are free to move among the groups and consult with students on request. A word of caution to teachers who choose this role: Students may use the consultant as the "final word" in settling disagreements among themselves or as the first resource to tap when looking for information on a topic. Students need to understand that disagreements should be worked out among the individuals involved and that the teacher should be consulted for information only after all other resources have been exhausted.

The *neutral* teaching role is used to promote independent thinking by students. Teachers assuming this role are the least active discussion group members. They remain silent by placing responsibility on the students for leading and contributing to discussions. Neutral teachers do not offer opinions, ask questions, or confirm responses. When students direct questions or responses to the neutral teacher, they are redirected to other students in the group. For teachers, the neutral role is an ultimate goal, because it marks the transfer of their modeled discussion behaviors to students.

Evaluating the success of a discussion

A critical aspect of planning for classroom discussion is knowing what did and what did not work in previous attempts. It is important for teachers to evaluate regularly the effectiveness of the discussion method. Decisions concerning evaluation are best made when planning a discussion. If teachers decide to evaluate verbal and nonverbal interaction patterns when their purpose for a discussion is to generate different points of view on an issue, they might use the bipolar evaluation of teacher-student interaction patterns. This holistic approach to evaluating classroom discussion enables teachers to generate profiles of personal effectiveness in using the discussion method for a specified instructional purpose. (A full description of the bipolar and other evaluation procedures is included in Chapter 7.)

Summary

Planning a discussion involves several steps: (1) specifying the overall instructional purpose for holding a discussion, plus identifying one or more lesson specific objectives; (2) analyzing the students' textbooks to select content amenable to the discussion method of teaching; (3) selecting appropriate content using different criteria for different instructional purposes; (4) selecting discussion strategies appropriate for a particular lesson; (5) organizing the classroom for either large or small group discussion, including the consideration of various teacher roles; and (6) planning in advance how a particular discussion's effectiveness will be judged.

References

Alvermann, D.E., Dillon, D.R., O'Brien, D.G., and Smith, L.C. The role of the textbook in discussion. *Journal of Reading*, 1985, *29*, 50-57.

Davidson, J.L. The group mapping activity for instruction in reading. *Journal of Reading*, 1982, *26*, 52-56.

Gage, N.L., and Berliner, D.C. *Educational psychology.* Chicago: Rand McNally, 1975.

Gall, M.D., and Gall, J.P. The discussion method. In N.L. Gage (Ed.), *Psychology of teaching methods.* National Society for the Study of Education, Seventy-Fifth Yearbook, Part I. Chicago: University of Chicago Press, 1976, 166-216.

Hill, W.F. *Learning thru discussion: A guide for leaders and members of group discussions.* Beverly Hills, CA: Sage, 1977.

Maier, N.R.F. *Problem-solving discussions and conferences: Leadership methods and skills.* New York: McGraw-Hill, 1963.

Manzo, A.V., and Casale, U.P. Listen-read-discuss: A content heuristic. *Journal of Reading,* 1985, *28,* 732-734.

McKeachie, W.J. *Teaching tips,* seventh edition. Lexington, MA: D.C. Heath, 1978.

Rudduck, J. (Ed.). *Learning to teach through discussion.* Norwich, England: University of East Anglia, Centre for Applied Research in Education, 1979.

Schallert, D., and Tierney, R. *Learning from expository text: The interaction of text structure with reader characteristics.* Contract No. NIE-G-79-0167. Austin, TX: University of Texas, 1982. (ED 221 833)

5

Discussion strategies
for content area reading

This chapter describes and provides examples of three discussion strategies to help students achieve subject mastery, examine several sides of an issue, or evaluate alternative solutions to a text based problem. Each strategy is matched to one of the instructional purposes for discussion outlined in Chapter 1. The purpose, rationale, and steps in implementing each strategy are followed by an example of its use in the content classroom and limitations are noted.

Listen-Read-Discuss

Purpose. The Listen-Read-Discuss (L-R-D) strategy is designed to expose students, through oral language, to the key concepts and basic facts found in their regularly assigned content area texts. Because L-R-D focuses on content learning, resembles the traditional Directed Reading Activity (DRA), and features the lecture method, it is most closely aligned with the instructional purposes of a subject mastery discussion. However, like most teaching strategies, L-R-D is not limited exclusively to subject mastery discussions.

Rationale. The L-R-D strategy reflects current theory, research, and practice. It affords students opportunities to build background knowledge, compare understanding of the lecture with understanding of the text, apply self-monitoring behaviors, and distinguish relevant (key concepts) from irrelevant information. During the discussion step of L-R-D, students are encouraged to clarify and elaborate on the same text they have been exposed to twice before—once during the teacher's lecture and once during the initial reading. The redundant features of this strategy enable students of lower reading ability to use three of their four senses in mastering the assigned content.

Steps for implementing L-R-D. The three basic steps to L-R-D are paraphrased here from an article by Manzo and Casale (1985).

1. To build students' confidence, the teacher should begin with a well structured portion of the required reading material that includes cues to that structure. For example, cause and effect structured text might include words like *because, as a result of,* or *therefore.* The teacher lectures on that portion of the text for about fifteen minutes.

2. The class then reads the pages on which the lecture was based. Students should be told to read for the purpose of comparing their understanding of the lecture with the information presented in the text. They might also read to locate words, ideas, or facts that are difficult to comprehend or inconsistent with the teacher's lecture.

3. Discussion follows. Initially, basic meanings should be clarified. After a more critical review of the material, students and teacher should raise some of the questions left unanswered by the text. Three questions help guide this discussion: What did you understand best from what you heard and read? What did you understand least from what you heard and read? What questions or thoughts did the topic raise in your mind? The order of the questions, the precise verbal form, and the number of questions asked will vary according to class needs, teacher inclinations, and the nature of the material.

Example of L-R-D. Ms. Hailey, an eighth grade earth science teacher, previewed a three page assignment on the topic of *matter.* Keeping in mind the average to above average reading ability of the students in her third period class, Hailey examined the text to determine what information was presented; how that information was structured or organized; and, finally, what misconceptions her students might have about *matter.* Since her major objective for this lesson was subject mastery, Hailey decided to use the L-R-D strategy.

She presented the key concepts in a structured overview on an overhead transparency. This structured overview helped her students to follow her fifteen minute lecture on *matter.* Next, the students spent fifteen minutes silently reading the three page assignment. Their purpose was to locate information that expanded on the lecture or appeared inconsistent with what Hailey had said about *matter.* Finally, students and teacher met as a large group to clarify, through discussion, any misconceptions generated from the lecture or the reading. Once students had demonstrated a basic understanding of the topic, the discussion turned to an examination of some of the unknowns surrounding *matter*.

The following is an excerpt from Hailey's class discussion.

Hailey
What did you understand best about matter from what you heard and read?

Sam
That matter means things that take up space.

Hailey
Okay, that's one definition of matter. What else? Mike?

Mike
Anything that has mass and takes up space.

Hailey
Okay, that's the definition given in your book. Can you, or someone else, give us some examples? (various ideas are shared by several students)

Hailey
What did you understand least about matter?

Julie
I don't get what isn't matter. Like, we can't see air, so it's not matter, right?

Several students (disagreeing with Julie)
But air takes up space.

Hailey
Julie, do you agree with that?

Julie
No...at least not if...no, I don't agree.

Jenny
All things take up space. Take blowing up a balloon, for example...(interrupted by teacher)

Hailey
What happens to your balloon? What's inside?

Julie (thinking, still looking puzzled)
Then there's nothing on earth that isn't matter?

Hailey
I can't think of anything, but maybe someone can. (teacher models a personal uncertainty)

Sam
Nope. (no one else volunteers a response)

Hailey
Well, what other questions or thoughts did this lesson raise in your mind about matter?

Mike
I'm still wondering about the matter of certain stuff—like the earth and air—what's it made up of?

Alvermann, Dillon, O'Brien

Jenny
Yeah, and how do scientists figure out what matter is made of?

Hailey
Those are both good questions. Let's read further to see if the author of our textbook answers them. If not, we'll talk about where we might go to find the answers.

At this point in the discussion, the students had generated their own purposes for reading the remainder of the article and the teacher assigned it as homework. The next class period began with a check to see if the answers to Mike's and Jenny's questions were found in the text.

Limitations. There are two major limitations of the L-R-D strategy: (1) There is a sizeable amount of repetition and students may be bored, and (2) the three basic steps of L-R-D do not allow for much student input. Teachers who use L-R-D may want to refer to adaptations suggested in the Manzo and Casale article.

The devil's advocate

Purpose. According to its inventor (Roby, 1983, p. 1), "The devil's advocate is a strategy for arguing against oneself in order to test the cogency of one's beliefs." When used appropriately, the devil's advocate is a powerful form of self criticism. Because it encourages students to look for the most convincing argument possible—one in direct opposition to the stance they have taken—the devil's advocate is especially well matched to the issue oriented discussion.

Rationale. The devil's advocate has a distinguished legacy, dating back to Plato's time. According to Roby (1983, p. 2), "In Book 2 of Plato's Republic, Galucon and Adeimantos put forth the best arguments for injustice, not because they believed them, but in order that Socrates be persuaded to make the strongest case for justice." In the devil's advocate, three results are possible: Individuals can strengthen their own positions after examining opposing positions; individuals can abandon their positions based on more compelling arguments of opposers; or individuals can modify their original positions by assimilating one or more of the objectives raised.

Steps for implementing the devil's advocate. One of the functions of the devil's advocate is to develop discussions in which the whole class is engaged in arguing against "self." The original question is best posed by the teacher the first few times. Once an issue has been chosen, the teacher invites pairs of students to disagree with themselves, and later, to switch positions. Next, the teacher asks individuals within the pairs to present their best arguments for each of the positions taken. Individuals also are encouraged to look at their positions for evidence of false reasoning. Originally, two positions may be all that students can handle, while later, three positions might become the minimum. After a few minutes the teacher initiates the "reflective turn." This technique involves asking students to describe how their participation in the devil's advocate strategy has changed their thinking. Finally, students are asked whether they have strengthened their position or have decided to abandon or modify it.

Example of the devil's advocate. Mr. Tennyson, a ninth grade social studies teacher, used the devil's advocate strategy to structure a class discussion on the banning of nuclear testing. His students had read a section of their text that dealt with the horrors of nuclear warfare. As the discussion opens, Tennyson has just finished assigning the students to pairs.

Tennyson
All right, now, you and your partner find a place where you can talk quietly. Each of you should jot down why you believe the United States should stop testing nuclear weapons. Be sure to support your beliefs with evidence from the text. Then take the opposite stance (why the United States should not stop testing nuclear weapons) and again support your beliefs with evidence from the text.

(The students, working individually in pairs, take about ten minutes to complete this task.)

Tennyson
Okay, now we're ready for the next step. Choose your best arguments (pro and con) and present them to your partner. Be certain that you discuss your beliefs with your partner; for example, seek your partner's ideas and evaluations of the pros and cons that you took on the issue. Is there evidence of any faulty reasoning on either one's part?

(After approximately fifteen minutes, the noise level in the room drops, an indication that students have finished presenting the arguments they had with themselves.)

Tennyson (standing by the chalkboard, pointing to some notes he had made)
May I have your attention....There are two more things I would like you to do: (1) Think about how your ideas have changed on banning nuclear testing. For example, has your position shifted from your original one? If so, why? (2) Decide whether you have strengthened your original position, abandoned it completely, or only modified it. Then tell your partner your decision and see if he or she agrees.

After approximately ten minutes, Tennyson drew the students into a whole class discussion by asking them to share some of their ideas on both sides of the issue. He was careful not to give the impression that he favored one side over the other. He did suggest that interested students should gather further evidence to support their final positions on the issue and promised to set aside some time for those students to report to the class.

Limitations. The devil's advocate frequently brings on a barrage of complaints from students when they are first encouraged to argue against themselves. The teacher may handle those complaints by reassuring the students that it is appropriate, even desirable, to look objectively at both sides of an issue. Initially, students tend to forget or prematurely switch their arguments. When this occurs, the teacher may find it beneficial to have students jot down their opposing arguments.

The developmental discussion

Purpose. The developmental discussion strategy was developed by Maier (1963) for the purpose of exposing students to the process of group problem solving. A problem, identified by the teacher in cooperation with the students, is divided into parts that must be resolved prior to solving the overall problem.

Rationale. The developmental discussion is a valuable strategy teachers can use to show how overall problems can be identified and then broken into more manageable parts. By interacting with their peers in small groups, students concurrently work through the problem solving process by using valuable reading comprehension skills. Students predict (hypothesize); they read and listen to confirm or reject their hypotheses; they gather evidence from the text and their own background knowledge to support possible solutions; and they use higher level thinking skills to evaluate the product of their efforts. Throughout the developmental discussion process, questions are raised for which answers are not already known. Often the hypotheses and solutions to the problem require application of information learned in earlier lectures and readings.

Steps for implementing the developmental discussion. Early in the developmental discussion process it is important that the problem be stated clearly and be understood by both teacher and students. Teachers can facilitate students' ability to formulate a text based problem by reviewing textbook and lecture content and modeling questions in a way that encourages students to use both their background knowledge and the information in their textbooks. For example, teachers might ask, "How does the idea that _____ apply to _____?" It is crucial that the students formulate a problem they are interested in solving. It is also important that they break the big problem into manageable parts.

After formulating the problem, students work in small groups to solve the smaller parts of that problem. Questions that guide their problem solving include:

- What do we know about this problem part?
- What information is relevant to the problem?
- What data do we need to construct a solution?
- What are some possible solutions?
- Which of these solutions are feasible based on what we know or what information we can gather?

After the small groups have completed their work on the common problem part, the teacher gathers the students for large group discussion. Students have the opportunity to observe the many ways one problem part can be solved along with the thinking behind the proposed solutions. Finally, the class as a whole sorts through the proposed solutions and either selects a solution (or combination of solutions) or decides to continue to search for further information before arriving at a solution. Eventually, a new problem part is identified, and the process begins again.

Example of developmental discussion. Mr. Freeble, a high school civics teacher, works with a group of average ability students for fifty minutes each morning. In a previous class session the students had read a five page textbook assignment and had completed the accompanying study guide. The assignment covered information about the Supreme Court—what it is, its purpose and charges, and its relationship to the entire governmental system.

Freeble began the developmental discussion by reviewing the previous textbook assignment for five minutes. From the review, students were reminded of the following key concepts: the Supreme Court is the highest court in the land, the individuals sitting on the Supreme Court are charged with interpreting the Constitution, and members of the Supreme Court may change a previous ruling by another branch of the government.

Next, Freeble asked the students to supply current information about events in the news concerning recent Supreme Court rulings. Elicited were facts about prayer in school and nativity scenes set up on public property. Freeble noted that the seasonal influence (it was close to Christmas) played a large role in students' interest in a local newspaper story about a controversial nativity scene. After ten minutes of discussing that story and its implications for local residents, the class decided on a problem that was text based but of immediate interest to them—should religious groups be allowed to erect nativity scenes on public property?

Alvermann, Dillon, O'Brien

The teacher guided the students in breaking the larger problem (separation of church and state) into three smaller problems: (1) Does setting up a nativity scene on public property violate the rights of individuals who do not have the same religious beliefs? (2) What information could the class add that would help solve the problem? (3) What would be a reasonable way to share what was learned with the people involved in the controversy?

The students broke into smaller groups and began to work on the first part of the problem. Freeble supplied each group with a one page summary of the Pawtucket case involving a Supreme Court ruling on the display of nativity scenes on public property. Freeble circulated among the groups, observing and offering assistance when requested.

During the last fifteen minutes of the period, students participated in a large group discussion in which they reported on their reactions to the Pawtucket case and whether they believed the case had any implications for the local controversy.

Over the next two days, the students worked in small groups to tackle the remaining problem parts. Solutions to the overall problem included working with community leaders to foster improved communication among the dissident groups and writing letters to the editor of the local newspaper on the topic of how the Pawtucket case compared to the local one.

Limitations. The success of the developmental discussion strategy depends on the selection of a textbook assignment that requires problem solving and on students being adept in using small group discussion skills. Teachers would not want to use this strategy without having worked with the discussion process. Teachers must be open to student selection of problems and problem parts as opposed to teacher selection of perhaps "better" problems or parts. Also, teachers must be willing to exchange their roles as information givers for discussion facilitators.

Summary

The discussion strategies in this chapter were designed to help students master the content of their assigned texts, examine both sides of an issue, and find a group solution to a text based problem. Each strategy was matched to an appropriate instructional purpose for discussion. The purpose and rationale, steps in implementing the strategy, an example of its use in the classroom, and a set of limitations surrounding its use were presented.

References

Maier, N.R.F. *Problem solving discussions and conferences: Leadership methods and skills.* New York: McGraw-Hill, 1963.

Manzo, A.V., and Casale, U.P. Listen-read-discuss: A content heuristic. *Journal of Reading,* 1985, *28,* 732-734.

Roby, T. *The other side of the question: Controversial turns, the devil's advocate, and reflective responses.* Paper presented at the annual meeting of the American Educational Research Association, Montreal, Canada, April 1983.

6

Implementing the discussion

C hapter 6 presents one content area teacher's implementation of a discussion he had planned covering the first chapter in Steinbeck's *Of Mice and Men*. This indepth examination of the discussion method, as defined by Mr. Appleby in his Basic English class, provides an opportunity to observe how the planning framework described in Chapter 4 was implemented in an actual classroom.

Commentaries that follow each of several segments of a videotape transcript taken from the discussion include an analysis of what happened during the discussion, how and why the teacher/student interactions proceeded as they did, and what changes in those interactions might be suggested to facilitate more effective discussions in the future.

Background information

Appleby's fifth period Basic English class met for fifty minutes daily. The class consisted of seventeen students (ten females and seven males) who were enrolled in grades ten through twelve. Their placement in Appleby's class was largely the result of their poor performance on the statewide criterion referenced test. The students, most of whom were black and from low socioeconomic backgrounds, were motivated learners despite their below average reading skills (Dillon, 1986).

Planning. Appleby planned a subject mastery discussion to monitor the students' understanding of the material and to make certain they got off to a good start. The discussion method was not new to Appleby, but his willingness to let the students read assigned materials on their own was new. Previously, he had read aloud almost all of the students' assignments as they followed along in their books (Alvermann et al., 1985). A specific objective in Appleby's planning was his desire to build the students' confidence in their ability to read and evaluate critically the motives and actions behind the main characters' thinking. He was careful to share with the class his overall purpose for holding the discussion prior to assigning Chapter 1 of the Steinbeck novel.

The discussion strategies Appleby chose to use with the class varied according to the students' responses and to demands of the content. The strategies are best described in the context of the commentaries. A question/study guide provided the overall framework for the discussion. The guide (see Figure) consisted of a structured overview, several multiple choice questions concerning difficult vocabulary in the story, and six comprehension questions. Appleby used the structured overview and vocabulary questions to build background for the novel. After reading Chapter 1 the first time, students were asked to reread parts of the chapter and answer the six comprehension questions for the next day's discussion.

Appleby's planning notes proved that he had given thought to how the class should be organized for the discussion. Because of the small class size and his wanting to lead the discussion of the questions on the study guide, Appleby selected the whole class discussion format. The desks in his classroom were permanently arranged in rows of two deep on two sides of the room, so students sat facing one another. Appleby stood at a lectern in the front of the room, halfway between the two groups of students.

Evaluation. Appleby continually assessed the effectiveness of the discussion method in helping his students critically evaluate what they had read. Through careful analysis of the transcribed videotape, we were able to isolate several instances in which his careful modeling of the desired behavior provided students with necessary motivation and skill to analyze the character traits of George and Lennie.

An analysis of a discussion

Of Mice and Men begins with Lennie and George traveling from the town of Weed to work on a ranch further south in the state of California. The men left Weed because of some trouble Lennie got into after he touched a girl's dress. Lennie is portrayed by the author as being a large, slow moving, mentally retarded man who loves to stroke soft things. George is Lennie's friend and self-appointed guardian.

The question/study guide*

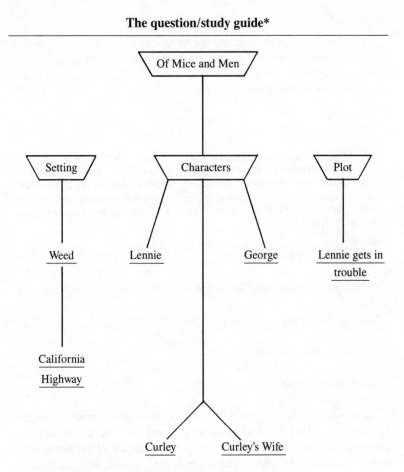

1. How does Steinbeck convey Lennie's animal like qualities?
2. Why does Steinbeck describe the actions of Lennie's hands?
3. What is George's attitude toward Lennie? Why does George stay with Lennie?
4. Explain the connection between Lennie's mouse and what happened in Weed.
5. Describe George's dream about life without Lennie.
6. Do you think George's dream is realistic?

* The vocabulary portion of the guide is not illustrated.

Segment 1

The first segment of the transcript begins with a review of the vocabulary in Chapter 1. The first person to talk is Andy, and his answer, *dominates*, is in response to Appleby's previous question, which does not appear on this portion of the transcript.

Andy
Dominates.

Appleby
O.K. If one football team dominates another, would they beat them bad? They would, wouldn't they? And take the trophy? All right, good! That's about as close as you need to get. They control something. So that's what George is doing. He's making Lennie give him the mouse. All right, *dejected* occurs on page 10; turn to that page. It has to do with Lennie—after he finally gives up his pet mouse. He's not happy, is he?

Students
No! (they begin to guess at answers)

Appleby
So the book says he sat down on the ground and hung his head dejectedly.

Students
A? B? C? (multiple choice guesses from their study guides)

Appleby
C is correct. Sad—that's good!

Ellen
Sad, he was so sad and lonely.

Commentary. During the review of the vocabulary words in context, Appleby controlled the discussion by eliciting student responses to his questions. He encouraged students to use their copies of the novel; however, he assumed the role of instructor while students were information givers. In future vocabulary review segments, Appleby might find it more advantageous to probe students' answers. Instead of letting students guess the right answers, he might help them discover why their choices are not appropriate.

Segment 2

When Appleby opened this segment of the discussion, he focused students' attention on the comprehension questions listed at the bottom of the study guide (see Figure). Students' answers came from what they remembered about the chapter; most had not taken notes.

Alvermann, Dillon, O'Brien

Appleby
The first question asks, How does Steinbeck convey Lennie's animal like qualities?

LaVonne
Like a bear walkin'.

Appleby
Walkin' like a bear.

Terry
Big hands and arms.

Appleby
Big hands and arms.

Ellen
Drinkin' like a horse! (Ellen laughs)

Appleby
Drinkin' like a horse – good! All of those things that he does not do verbally...

Ellen (interrupting)
He slurps his water! (Ellen laughs)

Appleby
All right, he slurps his water. How does he eat his beans?

Marty
With catsup? No! Wait! He slobbers them all over his mouth.

Appleby
He smears them all over his face, doesn't he?

Students
(several students talk at once, voicing their agreement)

Appleby
Yeah, like a baby! So that's almost like an animal, too. All right, good! Now, why do you think it is important, even after reading one chapter, that we know Lennie's size?

Marty
That he's real big!

Ellen
He is a giant!

Students
(other students voice their opinions)

Appleby
Okay, he's a big man – a giant of a man. Not only is he large, but what about the way he moves around?

Ellen
He's so big he can't move.

Commentary. In this second portion of the discussion transcript, Appleby attempted to elicit students' responses to his questions by indiscriminantly accepting all of their contributions. Acceptance was reflected in his praising of students and in his repeating their words. Because Appleby had as one of his specific objectives "less teacher talk and more active involvement of students," he did not call attention to inaccurate responses, but in future discussions, he might point out the discrepancies between his questions and the students' answers. With some refocusing on Appleby's part and some elaboration on students' parts, answers that were initially incorrect or incomplete could be molded into useful contributions.

Segment 3

In this segment of the discussion, Appleby emphasized the importance of the size of Lennie's hands to the story.

Appleby
Question two is going to connect with all the others. Why does Steinbeck describe the actions of Lennie's hands?

Marty
'Cause he killed that rat!

Appleby
All right, there's a good reason.

Ellen
He has power, more than he thought he had.

Appleby
All right, so what Ellen's saying is that...

Marty (interrupting)
He don't know his strength.

Appleby
Ah, very good! He doesn't know his strength, and Ellen also pointed out that he doesn't know his own power. Did he mean to kill the mouse?

Several students
No!

Ellen
He loved the mouse!

Appleby
He loved petting the mouse, didn't he?

Several students
Yeah!

Appleby
But all the mouse did was just nip a little bit. And obviously, being as big as Lennie was, did that hurt him?

Alvermann, Dillon, O'Brien

Several students
No, uh-uh.

Appleby
No, it didn't hurt bad. It made Lennie a little angry. And one pinch of his fingers and that was it for the mouse! What else did Lennie do with his hands that the author talked to us about?

Commentary. Appleby continued in his role as instructor, but was able to keep student participation lively and spontaneous by his willingness to let students interrupt him and also by his ability to model attributes of a good discussion. Appleby also modeled the importance of focusing on relevant information when he brought the group back to the topic of Lennie's hands. He did this without inhibiting students' remarks about Lennie's killing of the mouse. In effect, Appleby gave his students practice in how to think and sort through information in small steps.

Segment 4

Student contributions continued to increase in this next segment of the transcript, but as different students began to contribute to the discussion, Ellen's aggressiveness increased.

Appleby
What is George's attitude toward Lennie? Why does George stay with Lennie? There are two parts to the question. Let's start with George's attitude toward Lennie.

Ellen (blurts out)
He doesn't know anything.

LaVonne
He admires him.

Appleby
All right, he admires him is one answer. Something else?

Andy
He...

Ellen (interrupting)
He hates him.

Andy
He likes him, but he gets in the way.

Appleby
All right, does he get in the way? Is he a pest? (addressed to Andy)

Ellen (answers in place of Andy)
He gets in the way too much!

Students
Yeah! Yes!

Appleby
Okay, how does George express that attitude?

Ellen
He curses him! (laughs)

Appleby
He curses him, doesn't he...

Ellen (interrupting)
Using terrible language and stuff!

Appleby
Is George mad at Lennie?

Students
Yeah.

Terry
He's frustrated with him.

Ellen
Shut up, Terry! (Perhaps upset that Terry has joined the discussion?)

Appleby
Ah, that's not a bad word right there, Terry. George is frustrated with Lennie, isn't he? Why is he frustrated? Just because he's...

Students (interrupting Appleby and talking all at once)
He's always doin' something wrong!

Commentary. In this segment of the discussion, Appleby appeared to be looking for a particular answer to the question, "What is George's attitude toward Lennie?" He guided the students' understanding of both sides of George's feelings—why George liked Lennie part of the time and disliked him the other part. Although the discussion is still dominated by the teacher, it is important to note that Appleby's questions required students to justify their responses. Appleby's reaction to Ellen was to ignore her, then to respond to her, and finally to ignore her again. Part of Appleby's reason for staying with the teacher as instructor role may have been to ensure that all students had an opportunity to respond.

Segment 5

During this portion of the discussion, Appleby finished probing the students about George's reasons for staying with Lennie. Note that Appleby has changed roles and is now playing the devil's advocate (see Chapter 5) to help students examine different sides of an issue.

Appleby
Does Lennie get George in trouble?

Alvermann, Dillon, O'Brien

Students (several responding at one time)
Yes. No. Yes. He has!

Appleby
Sure he did—over the weekend.

LaVonne
Because they had lost so many jobs.

Appleby
All right! There's another good point. Also Lennie forgets things. He can't remember stuff that George tries to help him understand. That won't do! So if you had to put it in a sentence, would you agree if I said Lennie is a pain?

Students
Yes. Yeah!

Appleby
A pain in the neck?

Students (getting excited)
Yeah!

Appleby
Like a little brother who wants to tag along all the time.

Students
(all nod or shout agreement)

Appleby
Okay, if he's a pain then, if you guys think you're so smart that you've got Lennie labeled as a pain, how come George is with him? (in a playful tone of voice)

Students (all talking at once)
'Cause Lennie needs him. 'Cause George doesn't know any better. (laughter)

Tony
If Lennie didn't have George, he wouldn't know how to do anything.

Appleby
All right, listen to this...

Ellen (interrupts)
Lennie's mind's not capable...

Tony (interrupts Ellen)
Hush up! (directed toward Ellen) Lennie wouldn't know how to do anything, he'd be just helpless.

Andy
And when they go apply for a job they often get it because of Lennie's strength.

Appleby
Ah hah! Okay! Where do they work—at IBM? In Athens, Georgia?

Students (laugh)
No!

Appleby
Okay, they need Lennie's strength because he's strong, isn't he? Okay, so he helps George with his work in a lot of ways and he helps George keep jobs, *maybe*. But

Implementing the Discussion

let's get back to what Tony said. I've got to keep asking; if Lennie is such a pain, why can't George walk away? I mean George could go play cards....

Students
(students interrupt and begin talking and arguing their points of view with their neighbors)

Appleby (to one student's response)
I don't know...maybe....

Ellen (to Appleby)
I just told you! (referring to the question of why George can't leave Lennie)

Marty (agreeing with Ellen)
I know it!

Appleby
All right, Ellen, let's hear it.

Ellen
Because Lennie don't know what he's doin'. Because he forgets even though he tries to remember.

Appleby
Doesn't George apologize to Lennie a couple of times? Doesn't he say, "Lennie, I didn't mean to be mean and take that mouse away, but it wasn't fresh."

Marty
He feels responsible for Lennie.

Melinda
'Cause he don't have nobody to take care of him.

Appleby
Okay, he feels responsible for him, doesn't he? Lennie says, "I'll just wander off into the hills" and George says, "Ah, someone would shoot you for a coyote." So George feels responsible and feels sorry for Lennie and you have to keep that in mind until the end of the book.

Commentary. In this segment of the transcript, there appeared to be more student to student interaction. Appleby was more successful in getting his students to think critically about what they had read. His use of the devil's advocate role to help students see both sides of the issue seemed to spark more critical reaction to the text than any other strategy. He also was able to model for his students how to persuade others to look at an issue from a different point of view. For example, he tried to sway others to his side by referring to the book as an authoritative source. "Doesn't George apologize to Lennie a couple of times? Doesn't he say, 'Lennie, I didn't mean to be mean and take that mouse away, but it wasn't fresh.'?" Another important comprehension skill that Appleby modeled for his students was the importance of linking information from earlier chapters in the book to later chapters. He called their attention to the author's use of foreshadowing: "So George feels responsible for Lennie—you'll see that several times—and you must keep that in mind until the end of the book."

A final comment on this segment of the manuscript: It is important to note that Appleby's devil's advocate role had one drawback. He did not inform students about his use of the strategy; consequently, students were unaware of how its use affected their reactions to what others said. In subsequent discussions, Appleby might focus more directly on the devil's advocate role in terms of how it forces one to look at both sides of an issue.

Segment 6

In this final segment of the discussion, Appleby focused on questions five and six of the study guide. He also attempted to build students' confidence in their ability to evaluate the logic of their own and others' ideas. How successful he was can be seen through the following dialogue.

Appleby
All right, question 5. Describe George's dream about life without Lennie. Melinda?

Melinda
That he could get jobs and have money and have a girl.

Appleby
Sure! Have a girl. What else?

Marty
Have a job.

Appleby
Have money?

Marty
Have $50 at the end of the month.

Appleby
Have $50 at the end of the month. What else?

Tony
Have whiskey and hang around the pool halls and play.

Appleby
Hang around and play pool—in a sense it's basically what life would be like without Lennie...

Ellen (interrupting)
It's like a rough stair.

Terry
A crystal stair!

Appleby

Oh, you're going back to the Langston Hughes poem we read awhile ago. That would be a good comparison. But George is still with Lennie...(Appleby breaks off in mid sentence). Okay, question 6—and this can be a yes/no/maybe—we really won't be able to answer it until later. But I want you to think about it. Do you think George's dream [of the farm] is realistic?

Lorie

Yes.

Appleby

All right, Lorie said yes, she thinks they could have a farm. Anybody disagree?

Marty

I do!

Appleby

Well, I'll disagree with you! All right let's both disagree. Did they have any money?

Students

No!

Appleby

How are they going to get a farm?

Students (all brainstorm at once)

Get a job! Save!

Appleby

Okay, maybe they could save some money, but do they have a place? I mean, they haven't said where the farm is going to be!"

Ellen

They could buy some land.

Marty

They don't plan on leavin' that dumb man (Lennie) no time soon? (insinuating that because they can't obtain or keep jobs, they won't be able to buy the farm)

Appleby

That's true, now George wants Lennie to go with him.

Marty

That dumb man is liable to mess it all up—keep them from getting jobs.

Appleby

That's true! Now Marty's arguing that Lennie keeps them from getting jobs.

Andy

No, Lennie helps George get jobs.

Appleby

All right, Andy says that Lennie helps George get jobs. What about that?

Marty

But he still gets them run out of town for doing something else!

Appleby

What are we going to do with Lennie? He's a good worker, but what did George tell him yesterday?

Teresa

That he's a loudmouth!

Andy

That he's (George) gonna bribe him...

Appleby (interrupting)

Give him a little bribe. George said, "If you keep your mouth shut and act right, I'll buy you a puppy." What do you think of that, Marty? Just keep him on jobs and bribe him with soft things?

Marty

I still disagree.

Appleby

You still disagree? So we haven't changed your mind? Well, we'll keep this question in mind because the next couple of chapters will help us decide whether George and Lennie's dream will come true.

Commentary. In this last segment of the transcript, several students who had not previously participated in the discussion began to contribute their ideas. Appleby appeared to release part of the responsibilities he had assumed in his teacher as instructor role. However, his attempt to build students' confidence in their ability to evaluate the logic of their own and others' ideas seemed to be premature. For instance, when he attempted to show the conflict in the two viewpoints of Marty and Andy, no student tried to evaluate the reasonableness of either Marty's or Andy's argument. Perhaps the students did not understand Appleby's request or did not have sufficient time to formulate their responses.

More disappointing than the students' inability or unwillingness to take Appleby's challenge to find the logic (or illogic) in their peers' arguments, however, was Appleby's decision not to explore Terry's thinking when he alluded to an earlier read Langston Hughes poem. It seemed to be an excellent opportunity to demonstrate the value of making an analogy between the two pieces of literature. On the positive side, Appleby used the last few minutes of class to motivate students to read further in *Of Mice and Men*. He helped them develop a purpose for reading the next chapter and stressed the importance of reading to confirm or reject predictions.

Summary

Chapter 6 documents how one content area teacher implemented a discussion to use with students in his Basic English class. By analyzing the transcript of a videotaped discussion of a Steinbeck novel, it was possible to demonstrate the interrelatedness of the discussion method of teaching and the students' motivation to comprehend text that was difficult for their reading level. Wherever possible, information from earlier chapters in this book was woven into the commentaries following each segment of the transcribed videotape. The resulting commentaries capture how one teacher's ability to model the appropriate discussion skills contributed to his students' understanding and enjoyment of a well known novel.

References

Alvermann, D.E., Hayes, D.A., Dillon, D.R., and Layton, K. *How classroom discussion affects students' critical reading behavior.* Unpublished manuscript, University of Georgia, 1985.

Dillon, D.R. Toward a partial theory of teaching style: A microethnography of a secondary teacher working with students having low reading ability. *Dissertation Abstracts International,* 1986, *47*(2), 481-A.

Steinbeck, J. *Of mice and men.* New York: Viking Press, 1965.

7

Two procedures for evaluating discussion

This chapter presents two procedures for informally evaluating classroom discussions – procedures teachers can use to "debug" their classroom of discussion glitches, those little quirks that keep discussion from functioning the way teachers would like it to function. The idea came from *The Soul of a New Machine* (Kidder, 1982). This book describes how, after months of designing a computer system, the developers of the diagnostic program get the last bugs out of the system by running a prototype of the program. Like the diagnostic program in Kidder's book, the procedures in this chapter permit a view of a working system – classroom discussion – so that teachers can see what bugs need to be worked out.

The expression "If we could see ourselves as others see us" is important to this chapter. Being able to see ourselves as others see us is not an easy task. Consider the routine activity that fills each day at school. Teachers do not see themselves as they teach, and even if they did, the picture seen would be so commonplace that they would not be able to really *see* what they were *looking* at. Educational anthropologist Frederick Erickson (cited in Spindler, 1982, p. 15), uses the term "making the familiar strange" to describe the perspective teachers would have to adopt to see something unique in what would otherwise seem commonplace.

Teachers can adopt such a perspective by looking objectively at the quality of students' contributions within the discussion framework created by the teacher. This holistic approach to evaluating discussion enables teachers to understand the dynamics of their own classroom interaction patterns and plan desired changes in those patterns. This approach also provides teachers with a descriptive means for analyzing different types of discussion activities that go on daily in their classrooms. Finally, because holistic evaluation procedures do not presume any special training on the part of the evaluator, teachers can adapt and use them with little effort.

Procedure 1: A bipolar evaluation

The first evaluation procedure is one designed to define a spectrum of possible categories containing activities you may or may not employ during discussion. There are two applications of the bipolar evaluation: to determine whether a specific activity is included in class discussions and to examine where the activity (if included) fits between the two poles. Remember, with the bipolar model no value should be assigned to either pole.

The categories that follow include bipolar components of teacher-student interaction patterns that occurred in the twenty-four content area classrooms we observed. Each category is divided into its bipolar parts, which are separated by a broken line. The extreme poles for each category resulted from our identification of teachers whom we considered to be opposites within the system. Activities listed under each extreme are likely to occur, but are not necessarily exclusive to each extreme. To use this procedure, look at all of the bipolar components to determine where your classroom discussion fits in the range between the extremes. Mark with an X where you see the fit (if there is a fit). It is possible that within a component you may be at one extreme or the other.

Category: Use of written material

Focus: How the textbook and other written materials are used relative to the discussion.

Direct use -------------------------------- *Indirect use*

Material in text is used to verify a point or refute an argument.	Information in the text is mentioned in passing.
Questions are asked from the text and answers are read or paraphrased from the text.	The text is referred to but is not consulted.

Category: Pacing

Focus: How the discussion leader attempts to regulate the tempo of the discussion or establish some sort of rhythm in the interaction among the discussants.

Variable ------------------------------------- *Stagnant*

Variety of questions are used to tap existing knowledge.	Questions and answers are restricted to one type of information (e.g., factual recall).

| Questions are rephrased for clarification. | Questions are repeated with no attempt to clarify. |
| Variety of tonal and verbal patterns are used to ask/answer questions or state an opinion. | Monotonic, patterned rhythm is used in asking/answering questions. |

Category: Control

Focus: How the discussion leader attempts to maintain a dominant position in deciding the course of a discussion.

Tight control ---------------------------- *Loose control*

Content to be covered is carefully preselected.	Only the general topic is preselected.
Deviations from selected content are not tolerated.	Discussants are permitted to stray from topic.
The amount of material to be covered is preplanned.	The amount of material varies according to the circumstances.

Category: Sustaining

Focus: How the discussion leader tries to maintain a discussion along a planned course.

Nurture --- *Nature*

Questions requiring critical thinking are asked to foster a variety of reactions/judgments.	Factual level questions are used to monitor who did or did not read an assignment.
Physical props, visuals, or verbal examples are available to clarify concepts.	Little use of props or other devices to clarify concepts.
Variety of reinforcement techniques are used to reward students for acceptable responses.	Students' responses are evaluated in a standard way but with an unclear intent (e.g., "okay" to reinforce or mark time).

Category: Sense of audience

Focus: How sensitive a speaker is to his/her listeners

Other conscious ------------------------ *Self centered*

| Teacher attempts to balance student participation. | Teacher directs attention to a favored group. |

Risk taking atmosphere encourages participation without fear of rejection.

Students unlikely to take risks because they perceive the teacher as an evaluator.

Students respond to other students and value their peers' comments.

Students participate to obtain teacher approval.

Making a profile from the bipolar evaluation

After locating where your discussion falls in the categories just listed, decide which bipolar components are most appropriate to your instructional purposes for holding a discussion. The obvious bias in the descriptors (e.g., Variable vs. Stagnant in the Pacing category) is not meant to imply that components listed at a particular end of the pole should always (or never) be employed. Sometimes they may be desirable for specific objectives. Having identified which components are most appropriate to your instructional purposes, list them on the left side of a sheet of paper under a column labeled *Current activities*. Make a second column to the right labeled *Possible activities to try.* Then list activities you are currently using under the appropriate components on the left side of the paper. Next, describe an activity you would like to do that is closer to the *opposite* pole. Write this activity under the appropriate component on the right side of the paper. The aim is to give your discussions a better balance. To illustrate, here is a profile constructed by a seventh grade science teacher whose instructional purpose for discussion was subject mastery.

Current activities	**Possible activities to try**
• Use of written material	• Use of written material
Information in text is mentioned in passing.	Give students discussion guides that refer to specific locations in the text where students may find information to verify material being discussed.
• Pacing	• Pacing
Questions and answers are usually at the factual recall level.	Ask fewer questions with attention given to students' ability to draw on previous readings and lab experiences in formulating their responses.

- Sustaining

  Students' responses to questions are usually evaluated with "okay" or "good."

- Sense of audience

  The same three or four students do most of the talking.

- Control

  Students are rarely permitted to stray from the topic, and no information other than school information is brought to bear on the content.

- Sustaining

  Use a variety of feedback forms including elaboration probes (Could you go further with that idea?) and nonverbal cues.

- Sense of audience

  Introduce students to cooperative learning techniques and small group work.

- Control

  Reserve a block of time each week in which no restrictions are set on the amount of material to be covered.

The bipolar evaluation procedure in a larger framework

The bipolar evaluation procedure is most valuable when it is viewed in relation to the information from the other chapters leading to this one. For example, changing instructional purposes also may change the bipolar components of interest, which, in turn, will lead to a change in activities. Because of the ease with which the different combinations of instructional purposes and bipolar components can be rearranged and recombined, the bipolar evaluation procedure is also useful as a planning tool. Finally, the bipolar evaluation procedure can be used to improve student participation in class discussions. The sustaining, sense of audience, and control categories are particularly helpful in this respect. When using the categories to move students along the continuum from one extreme to the other, it is essential they know the teacher's reasons for the move and how they will benefit. Of equal importance is keeping students informed of their progress during the move. Since the bipolar evaluation profile lends itself well to visual inspection, teachers might consider using it to chart the growth a class makes toward improved participation in discussions. Individuals should not be singled out on the chart.

Procedure 2: Evaluation of discussion activities

The evaluation of discussion activities procedure is useful for analyzing discussions that follow content reading assignments. Instead of looking at opposite poles within categories, the focus is on a series of discussion activities. For each activity, the purpose is described, the problems posed for critical reading and thinking are explored, and suggestions for improvement are provided.

1. Teacher assigns reading from the textbook and follows up with a series of questions and answers.

Purpose. Reading assignments followed by question and answer sessions are often used to monitor who read an assignment or to provide a quick review of material already introduced.

Problems. The overuse of question and answer sessions may indicate that too much time is spent "testing" compared to teaching students how to think and react critically to what they have read. Also, by relying solely on the text and the author's questions, the level of interaction may be limited and, to an extent, dictated by the textbook author.

Solutions. Eliminate question and answer sessions of the round robin variety, replacing them with discussions in which students are encouraged to do more talking. In the following example, an eighth grade literature teacher checks students' understanding of the major events in the story and then challenges them to think critically about what they have read.

Teacher
The way we're going to go about it is I'll ask a few of you some questions and see what happens. But first, somebody summarize all the events.

Paula
(summarizes the story, *Antaeus*)

Teacher
Who does the author want you to think is the leader of the gang when the story starts?

Students
(Several students respond at once. Some tell their neighbors; others compete for the teacher's attention.)

Teacher (after listening and responding nonverbally to a few students' ideas)
But who winds up as leader?

Students (several voices heard at once)
TJ.

Teacher
    If you figure that TJ winds up as leader of the gang, what do you think is the
relationship between him and this Greek guy Antaeus?

    Two important complementary skills are evident in this approach: the
ability to summarize the important information, and the ability to think
critically about the summarized information. An appropriate strategy for
fostering this alternative approach to the more common recitation like
question and answer session is REAP (Read, Encode, Annotate, Ponder),
developed by Eanet and Manzo (1976). The strategy was originally intended for individual use as a study method, but it is easily adapted to the
discussion method.
    In the sample dialogue from the lesson on *Antaeus,* the first step (*read*)
had been completed as homework. The teacher began the discussion of the
story the next day by asking students to *encode* the author's ideas in their
own words. The *annotation* was the oral summary that Paula produced.
After clarifying a couple of points in Paula's summary, the teacher moved
students into the *ponder* stage by asking a question that required them to
think critically about the relationship between the leader of the gang and
Antaeus.

2. Teacher gives guidance and refocuses the discussion when necessary

    Purpose. When students are enthused about a topic, it is not unusual
for a chain reaction to occur in which one comment triggers another, and
so on. This spontaneity often results in deviation from the intended topic,
and teachers who see students straying too far from the topic often attempt
to refocus the discussion. Ideally, refocusing should maintain the direction
of the discussion but not inhibit student input.
    Problems. Because of outside pressures to cover a certain amount of
content within a given period of time, refocusing may be used to force
students to attend to a particular segment of the text at the expense of all
other content. When this occurs, students' spontaneity is curbed. Eventually, students believe the teacher is not really interested in their ability to
bring in outside information to support their answers, and a valuable critical reading skill is lost in the process.
    Solutions. Outside constraints can be managed by allotting certain
amounts of time for certain types of interactions. On days when the goal is
to cover as much material as possible, fast paced question and answer ses-

sions (recitations) might be used. This form of interaction has built-in controls that automatically refocus students' attention each time a new question is introduced. Lectures interspersed with thoughtful questions also can be used when time is at a premium. However, it is essential to set aside some class time for discussions that promote critical evaluation of what was read and provide opportunities for students to digress from a topic. Careful planning of available time can eliminate some of the frustration teachers and students experience when discussions are attempted but not enough time is allocated for them to be successful. Teachers who use alternatives to discussion should alert students to the purpose of each type of interaction (e.g., why question and answer sessions are more suited to some days' objectives than to others). Reserving the term *discussion* for interactions that truly are discussions will eliminate some of the resentment that builds when teachers refocus student talk during what students *perceive* to be an open discussion.

3. Teacher constructs a variety of questions designed to elicit a variety of responses during discussion

Purpose. Teachers interested in eliciting a variety of responses and in exploring a topic to some depth construct questions that assist students in making critical judgments about what they read. From a "levels" perspective (Herber, 1978; Pearson & Johnson, 1978), variety means using literal (textually explicit), interpretive (textually implicit), and applied (scriptally implicit) level questions. Asking a variety of questions is based on the notion that students think only in ways teachers ask them to think. While intuitively appealing, this notion is not without its critics. Consequently, teachers who pose multilevel questions need to instruct students in how to discuss them.

Problems. Research has shown that only half of the responses students generate match the cognitive level of the teacher's question (Dillon, 1982). From one third to one half of the incongruent responses fall below the cognitive level of the teacher's question. The use of multilevel questions imposes an unfair burden on students if they are allowed little time in which to formulate their answers or little direction on where to find the answers. Also, too many questions of any kind can foil a discussion and turn it into a recitation.

Solutions. Teachers can improve discussion in their content area classes by reducing the number of questions they ask, providing additional wait time, and guiding students on where to look for answers. According to

Dillon (1984, p. 55), "a single, well formulated question is sufficient for an hour's discussion." Regarding wait time, Rowe (1974) found that most teachers wait only one second before repeating a question or moving on to the next student. Some research has shown that if teachers would wait several seconds, students' engagement rate and length of responses would increase correspondingly (Swift & Gooding, 1983; Tobin & Capie, 1982). Raphael and Pearson (1982) developed a procedure for guiding students on where to look for answers. In their procedure, students are taught the distinction between sources of information needed to answer questions. A clear distinction is made between information in the text and information in a person's head (background of experiences) that can be used to answer a question. These question answer relationships (QARs) give readers a strategy they can use independently to find answers to textbook questions.

Summary

The two procedures for evaluating discussion that were presented in this chapter are based on actual classroom experiences. The first procedure, a bipolar evaluation of activities that change according to one's instructional purpose for holding a discussion, can be used by teachers to develop profiles of their interaction patterns with students. The second procedure is useful for analyzing discussion activities that teachers use as follow ups to assigned content area reading. The purpose is described, the problems the activity poses are explored, and some suggestions for solving those problems are provided.

References

Dillon, J.T. Cognitive correspondence between question/statement and response. *American Educational Research Journal*, 1982, *19*, 540-551.

Dillon, J.T. Research on questioning and discussion. *Educational Leadership*, 1984, *42*, 50-56.

Eanet, M.G., and Manzo, A.T. REAP: A strategy for improving reading/writing/study skills. *Journal of Reading*, 1976, *19*, 647-652.

Herber, H.L. *Teaching reading in content areas*, second edition. Englewood Cliffs, NJ: Prentice-Hall, 1978.

Kidder, T. *The soul of a new machine*. New York: Avon, 1982.

Pearson, P.D., and Johnson, D. *Teaching reading comprehension*. New York: Holt, Rinehart and Winston, 1978.

Raphael, T.E., and Pearson, P.D. *The effects of metacognitive strategy training on students' question answering behavior.* Technical Report No. 238. Urbana, IL: University of Illinois, Center for the Study of Reading, 1982.

Rowe, M.B. Wait time and rewards as instructional variables: Their influence on language, logic, and fate control, Part 1. *Journal of Research in Science Teaching,* 1974, *11,* 81-94.

Spindler, G. Editorial comment. In G. Spindler (Ed.), *Doing the ethnography of schooling.* New York: Holt, Rinehart and Winston, 1982, 15-18.

Swift, J.N., and Gooding, C.T. Interaction of wait time feedback and questioning instruction on middle school science teaching. *Journal of Research in Science Teaching,* 1983, *20,* 721-730.

Tobin, K.G., and Capie, W. Relationships between classroom process variables and middle school science achievement. *Journal of Educational Psychology,* 1982, *74,* 441-454.